BOTS &BYTES

BOTS &BYTES

AN INTRODUCTION TO **ARTIFICIAL INTELLIGENCE,**
ChatGPT, AND **MACHINE LEARNING**

JOHN BINKS

Bots & Bytes: An Introduction to Artificial Intelligence, ChatGPT, and Machine Learning

For more information, email John@Binks.net.

ISBN: 9798859070527

TABLE OF CONTENTS

FOREWORD
Before the Bots Take Over the World... or My Toaster vii

INTRODUCTION I

CHAPTER I
"Hello, Computer!" – The Dawn of Intelligent Machines 5

CHAPTER 2
"Brains, Not Just Metal" – The Basic Principles of Artificial Intelligence 14

CHAPTER 3
"More Than Just Ones and Zeros" – Introduction to Machine Learning 19

CHAPTER 4
"A Chat with ChatGPT" – Understanding Conversational
Artificial Intelligence.. 25

CHAPTER 5
"The Neurons in Artificial Brains" – The Basics of Neural Networks 33

CHAPTER 6
"Teachable Moments" – How Machine Learning (ML) Models Train 39

CHAPTER 7

"The Ethics Drive" – Moral and Societal Implications of Artificial
Intelligence (AI) 44

CHAPTER 8

"Mistakes and Gigabytes" – When Artificial Intelligence Goes Wrong 52

CHAPTER 9

"Silicon Tycoons"- The Gold Rush of AI 56

CHAPTER 10

"AI Around the World"- A Whistle-Stop Tour of Global Ambitions 60

CHAPTER 11

"Into the Artificial Intelligence (AI)Verse" –
Real-world Applications and Examples 67

CHAPTER 12

"Future Bytes" – What Lies Ahead for Artificial Intelligence,
ChatGPT, and Machine Learning 75

EPILOGUE

"Artificial Intelligence, Humans, and the Age-Old
Quest for the Off Switch" 81

IN CONCLUSION: 86

APPENDIX

Key Terms and Definitions 87

ACKNOWLEDGMENTS

An Ode to Humans, Machines, and That Stubborn Wi-Fi Signal 93

BEFORE THE BOTS TAKE OVER THE WORLD... OR MY TOASTER

Ah, the wonders of the 21st Century! We're at a peculiar junction where my refrigerator can text me about low milk levels, and your coffee maker probably knows more about your morning moods than your partner does. Artificial Intelligence (AI) is sprinkled everywhere, from the trending videos on our social feeds to the uncanny way our phones autocorrect to words we didn't even know we wanted (or did we?).

When I first started *Bots & Bytes: An Introduction to Artificial Intelligence, ChatGPT, and Machine Learning,* I had two distinct thoughts. I wondered if reading this would finally let me win an argument against my home's intelligent assistant. The second was whether I'd understand a word beyond "Hello, Computer!"

But, oh, how this delightful tome proved me wrong!

Here, we have a book that doesn't just regurgitate a buffet of tech jargon. Instead, it unwraps the Artificial Intelligence (AI) conundrum with the zest of someone peeling a particularly juicy orange, ensuring every segment is as delectable as the next. The chapters within these pages don't merely talk at you; they converse, jest, and sometimes even share a digital wink (I'm convinced of it).

From humorous takes on why robots might want to grace school hallways (no, not to become prom king) to the quintessential debate on robot friendships (who wouldn't want a buddy that reminds you of birthdays and doesn't eat the last slice of pizza?), this book covers it all. It's a symphony of stories, analogies, and light-hearted banter that makes the complex world of one's and zero's understandable and utterly fascinating.

Bots & Bytes: An Introduction to Artificial Intelligence, ChatGPT, and Machine Learning is not just a guide—it's an experience. It nudges you to contemplate, chuckle, and perhaps even converse with your tech gadgets a tad kindlier. Because, let's face it, you never know when your toaster might want a day off or, heaven forbid, join forces with the blender!

So, as you delve into the depths of this book, I hope you find enlightenment, entertainment, and perhaps a new appreciation for the tech that hums quietly (or loudly, if it's that old PC of yours) in the corners of your life.

Remember, in the vast sea of technology, it's always better to ride the waves than to get caught in the undertow. Happy reading, and may your Wi-Fi always remain strong!

- An Enthusiastic Human and Occasional Debater with Voice Assistants

INTRODUCTION

Hello, dear reader! If you've picked up this book, chances are you've either been fascinated by the promise of Artificial Intelligence (AI) shown in movies, been baffled by a news report about robots doing human jobs, or wondered what on Earth your tech-savvy friend means when they say, "I trained a new model today!" Let me assure you that whichever camp you fall into – you're in for a wild, enlightening, and occasionally chuckle-worthy ride. Welcome to the ever-evolving world of *Bots & Bytes: An Introduction to Artificial Intelligence, ChatGPT, and Machine Learning.*

Let's set the scene. Imagine, for a second, a world where you have an army of tireless workers. They don't sleep, they don't eat, and they certainly don't request vacation days. They're perfect. Well, they are, until one of them mistakes a banana for a toaster or composes a love song when you ask for a lullaby. Those little eccentricities. That's Artificial Intelligence (AI) in all its flawed, fascinating glory.

Artificial Intelligence (AI) isn't just about robots taking over the world (despite what Hollywood might have you believe). It's also about understanding patterns, making decisions, learning, and adapting. In the following pages, we will demystify this world of ones and zeros, diving deep into the mechanisms that power these systems, their genius blunders' (and occasional hilarity), and the profound ways they're reshaping our world.

Our journey begins in Chapter 1, where we reflect on Artificial Intelligence's (AI) impact on popular culture, our hopes and fears, from Star Trek's omnipresent computer to early sci-fi visionaries' dreams (and nightmares). Are you ready to separate the myth from reality?

Have you ever wondered what makes Artificial Intelligence (AI) different from the software running your washing machine? In Chapter 2, "Brains, Not Just Metal" – The Basic Principles of Artificial Intelligence (AI), we'll delve into that. Trust me; it's not about the robot uprising (yet) but more about how machines are shifting from mere rule-followers to dynamic learners.

Chapter 3 promises to be a joyride through the intriguing world of Machine Learning (ML). We'll discuss why training a machine is like teaching your dog to fetch... but without the wet, slobbery tennis ball at the end.

Chatbots have increasingly become the digital face of many businesses, and in Chapter 4, we'll have a heart-to-heart with one of the most advanced of them all - ChatGPT. Spoiler alert: If ChatGPT had a dating profile, it might be the wittiest one out there!

Have you ever heard the term "Neural Network" and imagined an intricate web of something technical? Fear not! In Chapter 5, we'll break it down, exploring how these "artificial brains" function and why an artificial neuron's "day at work" might be more relatable than you think.

As we roll into Chapter 6, we'll see how machines like us have their own "teachable moments." It's not about apples falling on heads but more about bytes, data, and feedback loops.

No story is complete without a touch of drama, and Artificial Intelligence (AI) has its share. Chapter 7 dives into the deep and sometimes murky waters of ethics in Artificial Intelligence (AI). Would you rally for robot rights or protest against them? Let's explore together.

Not everything is rosy in the Artificial Intelligence (AI) world. Machines mess up, often in ways that are hilarious to us humans. Chapter 8 we will revisit some of the most epic (and comedic) Artificial Intelligence (AI) failures. But remember, these blunders often lead to the most profound advancements.

In Chapter 9, we'll delve into a narrative as enthralling as a telenovela, navigating the 21st century's Artificial Intelligence (AI) Gold Rush. Echoing the California Gold Rush of 1849, Silicon Valley giants and newcomers alike are wielding their virtual pickaxes, vying to capitalize on this digital treasure.

We invite you, our tech-savvy explorers, to strap in for a whirlwind voyage across the globe's Artificial Intelligence (AI) landscape without leaving the comfort of your seat. In Chapter 10, prepare to navigate the intricate tapestry of global Artificial Intelligence (AI) ambitions and ensure those logic gates are securely fastened!

The real world is where the rubber meets the road. In Chapter 11, we will uncover how Artificial Intelligence (AI) touches everything from diagnosing diseases to recommending your next binge-worthy show. And yes, people have asked voice assistants some genuinely bizarre things!

Finally, as we gaze into our digital crystal ball in Chapter 12, we'll try to discern the future of Artificial Intelligence (AI), ChatGPT, and Machine Learning (ML). The future might be uncertain, but one thing's for sure - it promises to be interesting.

So, whether you're a curious soul, an aspiring tech whiz, or someone just trying to keep up with the digital Joneses, this book is your ticket to understanding one of the most transformative forces of our age. Let's embark on this journey together with a mix of wisdom, wonder, and wit. After all, in *Bots & Bytes: An Introduction to Artificial Intelligence, ChatGPT, and Machine Learning*, there's always room for a little byte of humor!

Now, without further ado, let's plug in and power up!

CHAPTER 1

"HELLO, COMPUTER!" – THE DAWN OF INTELLIGENT MACHINES

Ah, the humble beginnings. Every epic tale, every groundbreaking discovery, every awe-inspiring invention – they all start somewhere. Just like the evolution of humankind from mere microbes to intellectual beings, the world of Artificial Intelligence (AI) has its origins, misconceptions, and a rich tapestry of tales. Let's journey back in time and explore the idea that laid the foundation for the mesmerizing realm of intelligent machines.

FROM FICTION TO REALITY: ARTIFICIAL INTELLIGENCE (AI) IN POP CULTURE

"Computer, locate Captain Kirk," said Spock as he confidently strolled through the deck of the Starship Enterprise. Sound familiar? Star Trek and other iconic science fiction productions embedded the idea of computers and machines that could think, converse, and make decisions long before they became a reality.

Movies and TV shows have always held a mirror to our societal aspirations and fears. In these fictional universes, intelligent machines were often portrayed in two extremes: benevolent companions like Star

Wars' R2-D2 or malevolent foes like the Terminator's Skynet. However, the essence of these portrayals has always been rooted in the complex relationship between humanity and its technological creations.

Fiction gave us a playground to imagine. In the pages of Isaac Asimov's tales or the frames of Stanley Kubrick's "2001: A Space Odyssey", we dared to envision a future where machines could potentially rival human intelligence. HAL 9000, the calm-speaking yet sinister computer in Kubrick's magnum opus, was a marvel of its time, a prescient example of the potential and pitfalls of Artificial Intelligence (AI). These tales, while exciting, were often exaggerated. But the inspiration they provided? Real.

THE REAL-WORLD DAWNING: WHEN FICTION MET FUNCTIONALITY

While sci-fi writers and filmmakers were busy sculpting Artificial Intelligence (AI) -driven worlds in their narratives, the natural world was just a little behind. The dawn of intelligent machines began in the ivory towers of academia and the hidden corridors of research facilities.

Remembering that the initial idea wasn't to create a machine that could mimic human emotions or plot world domination is essential. The primary goal was to simulate certain human problem-solving features in devices. Artificial Intelligence (AI)'s roots can be traced back to ancient history, where philosophers mused about the idea of artificial beings. However, it was in the 20th Century that things indeed took shape.

In the 1950s, computer scientist Alan Turing posed a simple yet profound question: "Can machines think?" This led to the development of the Turing Test – a method to determine whether a machine's intelligence could match or be indistinguishable from human intelligence. This idea was revolutionary. It bridged the world of abstract philosophical inquiries with the tangible realm of engineering.

The 1956 Dartmouth Workshop is another significant milestone. Here, pioneers like John McCarthy, who coined the term "Artificial Intelligence" in 1956, Marvin Minsky, and Claude Shannon, to name a few, gathered to jump-start the Artificial Intelligence (AI) field. They were optimistic, thinking a summer's effort could make significant headway. While their optimism was a tad premature, their passion and dedication laid the groundwork for the discipline's future.

Artificial Intelligence (AI) Development History Timeline

EARLY PREDICTIONS: THE HUMOROUS SIDE OF FORECASTING THE FUTURE

Predicting the future is a tricky business. In the initial excitement surrounding Artificial Intelligence (AI), there were many lofty predictions, some of which missed the mark by a country mile. For instance, Marvin Minsky, a leading figure in the Artificial Intelligence (AI) realm, once proclaimed in the 1960s that the problem of creating "Artificial Intelligence" would be substantially solved within a generation. Oh, Marvin, if only you knew!

Then there was the rather humorous prediction by Herbert A. Simon, who boldly stated in 1965, "Machines will be capable, within twenty years of doing any work a man can do." Well, we're still waiting!

These missteps in predictions highlight the unpredictability of innovation. These pioneers were optimistic; they just underestimated the complexities involved. And while these statements might seem humorous now, they reflect the enthusiasm and conviction of the era.

THE REALITY CHECK: PEAKS AND VALLEYS OF THE ARTIFICIAL INTELLIGENCE (AI) EVOLUTION

Artificial Intelligence (AI)'s journey has been a challenging, upward trajectory like any great story. There have been peaks of profound achievements and valleys of stagnation.

The 1960s and 70s witnessed the first wave of Artificial Intelligence (AI) enthusiasm, backed by substantial funding and interest. However, as the challenges became apparent and the initial predictions fell flat, we entered the first "Artificial Intelligence (AI) winter" in the late 70s, a period of reduced funding and waned interest.

The cycle repeated with a renewed interest in the 1980s, especially around expert systems – computer programs that mimic the decision-making abilities of a human expert. But again, as limitations emerged, another Artificial Intelligence (AI) winter ensued in the late 80s and 90s.

These fluctuations might seem disheartening, but they served a crucial purpose. They sifted out the hype from reality and paved the way for genuine, albeit slow, progress.

THE MODERN RENAISSANCE: ARTIFICIAL INTELLIGENCE (AI)'S RESURGENCE IN THE 21ST CENTURY

Post the 1990s, Artificial Intelligence (AI) witnessed a renaissance as computational power grew and data became the new oil. Techniques that were once deemed theoretical became practical. The buzzword of this era? Neural Networks and Deep Learning. But more on that in a later chapter.

What's important to note is that today's Artificial Intelligence (AI), while impressive, is still a far cry from the sentient beings of our fictional tales. Siri might be able to set a reminder or play your favorite song, but she's still light-years away from HAL 9000's multifaceted capabilities (and that might be a good thing!).

FROM ART TO IMAGERY: THE POWER OF GENERATIVE ARTIFICIAL INTELLIGENCE (GAI) AND GENERATIVE ADVERSARIAL NETWORK (GAN)

Generative Artificial Intelligence (GAI) refers to a subset of Artificial Intelligence (AI) systems capable of creating new, previously unseen content, patterns, or data. Rather than being designed to respond to inputs in predictable ways or make decisions based on data it's been trained on, a Generative Artificial Intelligence (GAI) system generates new outputs, whether that's images, text, music, or even complex patterns. One of the most well-known techniques in Generative Artificial Intelligence (GAI) is the Generative Adversarial Network (GAN), where two Neural Networks (the generator and the discriminator) "compete" in a kind of game, ultimately honing the generator's ability to produce realistic outputs. Whether crafting a new artwork, writing a piece of music, or even creating a realistic-looking photograph of a non-existent person, Generative Artificial Intelligence (GAI) pushes the boundaries of what machines can create.

FROM SPECIALIZED TASKS TO HUMAN-LIKE INTELLECT: A DIVE INTO ARTIFICIAL GENERAL INTELLIGENCE (AGI) AND NARROW ARTIFICIAL INTELLIGENCE (NAI)

Artificial General Intelligence (AGI) refers to a type of Artificial Intelligence (AI) that can understand, learn, and apply knowledge in a wide variety of tasks at a level comparable to human intelligence. Unlike Narrow Artificial Intelligence (NAI) (which is designed to perform a specific task), Artificial General Intelligence (AGI) can theoretically perform any intellectual task that a human being can. Achieving Artificial General Intelligence (AGI) is a major goal in the field of Artificial Intelligence (AI) research.

Narrow Artificial Intelligence (NAI), also known as Specialized or Weak Artificial Intelligence (AI), refers to Artificial Intelligence (AI) systems that are designed and trained for a specific task. Unlike Artificial General Intelligence (AGI), which has broad capabilities comparable to human intelligence, Narrow Artificial Intelligence (NAI) operates under a predefined set or context and doesn't possess general problem-solving capabilities.

Examples of Narrow Artificial Intelligence (NAI) are abundant in our daily lives. They include:

- Search engines like Google
- Voice assistants like Siri or Alexa
- Recommendation systems on platforms like Netflix or YouTube
- Image recognition software

These systems are very good at the specific tasks they're designed for, but they lack the ability to perform tasks outside of that specific domain.

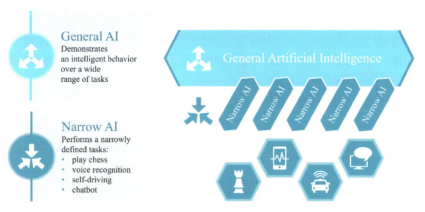

Types of Artificial Intelligence – General versus Narrow AI

MOORE'S LAW AND ITS RENDEZVOUS WITH ARTIFICIAL INTELLIGENCE (AI)

Ah, Moore's Law, that good ol' prophecy from Gordon Moore, which has been the tech equivalent of the North Star for the better part of the computing era. As you know, the observation suggests that the number of transistors we can cram onto a chip will double approximately every two years. But what happens when this technological titan meets the bustling bazaar of Artificial Intelligence (AI)? Let's dive in!

For starters, the breakneck speed of improvements in computing power—thanks to Moore's Law—has been a wind beneath Artificial Intelligence (AI)'s wings. This consistent growth has allowed researchers to handle larger datasets, build more complex models, and run computations that were once deemed the stuff of fantasy. Remember, just a few decades ago, voice recognition was as finicky as a cat deciding whether to stay in or out. Now? Your voice assistant probably knows your pizza topping preferences better than your best friend!

Moore's Law also made Artificial Intelligence (AI) research more accessible. As computational power became cheaper, more individuals and companies could jump into the Artificial Intelligence (AI) fray, leading to a democratization of innovation. Instead of a few bigwigs holding all the Artificial Intelligence (AI) cards, we had underdogs and start-ups tossing their hats into the ring.

However, it hasn't all been sunshine and algorithmic rainbows. The continued reliance on Moore's Law has also presented challenges for Artificial Intelligence (AI). As we approach the physical limits of silicon-based chips, some Artificial Intelligence (AI) computations have started to hunger for more power than the law can provide. This has led to two exciting trends:

- **Hardware Innovations for Artificial Intelligence (AI):** Recognizing that Moore's Law alone won't quench Artificial Intelligence (AI)'s thirst for power, there's been a surge in specialized hardware, like Tensor Processing Units (TPUs) and other Application-Specific Integrated Circuits (ASICs). These tools are tailor-made to handle Artificial Intelligence (AI) computations efficiently.

- **Algorithmic Improvements:** The onus has shifted towards making algorithms leaner and meaner, ensuring that Artificial Intelligence (AI) models run effectively without guzzling computational power.

In essence, while Moore's Law has given Artificial Intelligence (AI) a rocket-powered skateboard, it's also nudged the field to think about the journey ahead, where roads might be rockier. As we hit potential speed bumps or detours in Moore's prophecy, the Artificial Intelligence (AI) community is gearing up, innovating, and ensuring that even if the skateboard slows, the momentum never does. So, here's to Moore's Law: the backstage pass that helped Artificial Intelligence (AI) rock the main stage and will undoubtedly continue to shape its encores!

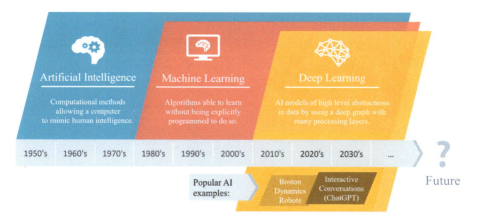

History Timeline of Artificial (AI), Machine Learning & Deep Learning

IN SUMMARY: IT'S JUST THE BEGINNING

The dawn of intelligent machines is filled with ambition, setbacks, humor, and profound achievements. From Hollywood's silver screens to MIT's labs, the journey of Artificial Intelligence (AI) is a testament to human ingenuity and perseverance.

As we continue our exploration in the upcoming chapters, remember this – Artificial Intelligence (AI) is as much a story about human dreams and aspirations as it is about circuits and algorithms. It's a field where fiction inspires reality and where every byte has the potential to revolutionize our world.

So, the next time you say, "Hello, Computer," to your voice assistant or marvel at a piece of tech that seems straight out of a sci-fi novel, take a moment to appreciate the incredible journey that brought it to life. And always remember, this is just the beginning. The horizon of Artificial Intelligence (AI) stretches far and wide, and we're here to explore it together. Onwards!

CHAPTER 2

"BRAINS, NOT JUST METAL" – THE BASIC PRINCIPLES OF ARTIFICIAL INTELLIGENCE

So, you've made it past the curtain-raiser, traversing the fascinating landscapes where computers first sparked conversations. But what's all the buzz about? What makes these machines seemingly "think"? Are they just rigid metal blocks, or is there something more—perhaps a semblance of a brain? Buckle up as we delve deeper into understanding the fundamentals that power these incredible systems.

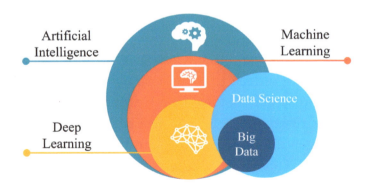

Embedding of Artificial (AI) Technologies

BEYOND THE METAL: THE HEART AND SOUL OF ARTIFICIAL INTELLIGENCE (AI)

To start, let's clear up a misconception. When we talk about Artificial Intelligence (AI), we're not referring to metallic robots with flashing lights, arms, and legs (even though that's what popular culture often showcases). Artificial Intelligence (AI), in its essence, is software. It's a series of algorithms that process information, learns, and make decisions based on that data. Think of it as the brain within the machine, even if the device is just a server in some cloud facility.

Still, why the comparison with brains? Because, in many ways, Artificial Intelligence (AI) systems are designed to mimic certain aspects of human cognition. The idea isn't to replicate the human brain in its entirety (that's an immense challenge that's still in the realms of sci-fi) but to emulate the way we recognize patterns, learn from experiences, and make decisions.

PRE-PROGRAMMED TASKS VS. LEARNING: THE KEY DISTINCTION

Now, it's essential to distinguish between Traditional Computing and Artificial Intelligence (AI) concepts. And yes, there's a world of difference.

- **Traditional Computing:** Picture this. You're at a vending machine, inputting a code to get a delicious candy bar. You press B4, and out pops your treat. This is a lot like traditional computing. You have specific instructions (the code) and an expected outcome (the candy). Computers have been doing this for decades, executing predefined tasks based on explicit instructions.

- **Artificial Intelligence (AI):** Now, imagine a different scenario. You're teaching a child to differentiate between other candy bars. Initially, they might mix up a Snickers with a Milky Way. But over

15

time, with more exposure and gentle corrections, they learn to distinguish them accurately. This process of learning from data and refining understanding is at the heart of Artificial Intelligence (AI).

While traditional computers strictly follow their programming, Artificial Intelligence (AI) systems are designed to learn from the data they're exposed to. They adapt, evolve, and improve over time. And just like you wouldn't expect a child to know algebra without prior exposure suddenly, an Artificial Intelligence (AI) system needs data, and lots of it, to perform its tasks efficiently.

THE UNDERLYING MAGIC: ALGORITHMS AT PLAY

Beneath the surface, algorithms drive the world of Artificial Intelligence (AI). Now, the word algorithm might sound intimidating, but at its core, it's just a fancy term for a series of steps or instructions designed to perform a particular task.

When you follow a recipe to bake a cake, you're following an algorithm. The difference is that in the Artificial Intelligence (AI) world, these algorithms deal with data—crunching numbers, recognizing patterns, making predictions, and so forth.

There are various types of algorithms, each suited for different tasks. Some are designed to sort information, others to find specific data within large datasets, and others, the ones we typically associate with Artificial Intelligence (AI), are meant to learn from data and improve over time.

TRAINING THE ARTIFICIAL INTELLIGENCE (AI): A CONTINUOUS JOURNEY

Training is one of the most vital processes in Artificial Intelligence (AI). Just as a student studies and practices to ace an exam, Artificial

Intelligence (AI) systems undergo training to perform their designated tasks efficiently.

This training involves feeding the Artificial Intelligence (AI) system vast amounts of data, allowing it to adjust its internal parameters (think of these as "beliefs" or "understanding") to improve performance. This iterative process—where the Artificial Intelligence (AI) system keeps adjusting and refining its knowledge based on new data and feedback—sets Artificial Intelligence (AI) apart from traditional computing.

For example, in image recognition tasks, an Artificial Intelligence (AI) model might initially mistake a picture of a cat for a dog. However, through iterative training and corrections, the system gradually gets better, learning the distinct features that differentiate cats from dogs, and eventually, it can identify them with high accuracy.

WHY THE EMPHASIS ON LEARNING?

The crux of Artificial Intelligence (AI) lies in its adaptability. In a rapidly changing world, static solutions often need to be updated. Artificial Intelligence (AI)'s power comes from its ability to evolve, adapt, and provide solutions even when faced with new scenarios or data it hasn't seen before. This adaptability is why Artificial Intelligence (AI) systems are now found in diverse fields, from healthcare diagnostics to financial forecasting and virtual assistants to self-driving cars.

IN SUMMARY: MORE THAN JUST TOOLS

Artificial Intelligence (AI) is more than just metal or lines of code. It's a confluence of data, algorithms, and the overarching principle of learning. The systems we create aren't just tools but extensions of our intellectual curiosity, exemplifying our desire to push boundaries and venture into the unknown.

Artificial Intelligence (AI) is a testament to our enduring spirit of innovation in the grand scheme. It's a field where mathematical rigor meets the abstract nuances of human cognition, where logic intertwines with intuition.

As we continue our journey through the intricacies of Artificial Intelligence (AI), always remember at the heart of these advanced systems lie principles inspired by and reflective of us—our brains, processes, and insatiable thirst for knowledge.

So, the next time someone mentions Artificial Intelligence (AI), think not of cold, unfeeling metal but of a dynamic, evolving brain—a brain that, while artificial, is brimming with potential and possibilities. Onward to the next chapter, where we'll dive into the fascinating world of Machine Learning (ML)!

CHAPTER 3

"MORE THAN JUST ONES AND ZEROS" – INTRODUCTION TO MACHINE LEARNING

"Machine learning is the study of computer algorithms that allow computer programs to automatically improve through experience."

- Tom M. Mitchell, Carnegie Mellon

Well, here we are. After whizzing through the realm of Artificial Intelligence (AI), it's time to delve deeper into a space that makes up the beating heart of most modern Artificial Intelligence (AI): Machine Learning (ML). Now, bear with us before you dash off to brew that cup of coffee (or grab a Coke Zero; we don't judge), fearing a tech avalanche. We promise this will be a fun, light-hearted, and (dare we say) relatable journey into the world of Machine Learning (ML)!

FIRST UP: WHAT IS MACHINE LEARNING (ML)?

At its core, Machine Learning (ML) is the science (and art) of allowing computers to learn from data and make decisions without being explicitly programmed for every scenario. It's a key pillar of Artificial Intelligence (AI) and why we can have meaningful conversations with virtual assistants, receive personalized movie recommendations, or even marvel at self-driving cars navigating bustling city streets.

Imagine teaching a child to differentiate between different fruits. You show them apples, oranges, and bananas. Over time, even without offering them every apple variety under the sun, they can confidently point one out at a market. This ability to generalize from examples is the essence of learning, and it is what Machine Learning (ML) models aim to do—with data!

FROM OUR WORLD TO MACHINE WORLD: A TALE OF DATA

Daily, we're surrounded by many experiences—sounds, sights, and tastes. For machines, this sensory bonanza translates to data. A photograph, for instance, becomes an array of pixel values. A piece of music transforms into waveform data. What are your online shopping habits? Yep, you guessed it, data again.

Everything Machine Learning (ML) does, from recognizing your voice to predicting stock market trends, is fueled by data. The better the quality and quantity of this data, the more accurately a Machine Learning (ML) system can perform its tasks.

TRAINING A DOG VS. TRAINING A MACHINE: NOT SO DIFFERENT AFTER ALL?

Humor us for a moment. Think about how you'd train a puppy. You'd show it where its food bowl is, where to find its bed, or how to fetch a ball. Each time the puppy does something right, you reward it—maybe with a treat or affection. When it gets things wrong (like mistaking your shoe for a chew toy), there's a corrective action.

Training a Machine Learning (ML) model is eerily similar. Here's how:

- **Input (The Scenario):** In the dog's world, this could be a thrown ball or a command to sit. In Machine Learning (ML), it's the data you provide—like a collection of pictures labeled "cat" or "not cat".

- **Output (The Reaction):** The dog might fetch the ball or plonk its furry behind down. After training, a Machine Learning (ML) model might look at a new picture and say, "That's definitely a cat!"

- **Feedback (Correction):** If the dog returns a stick instead of the ball, you will correct it. If your Machine Learning (ML) model sees a raccoon picture and goes, "Oh, a fluffy cat!" It needs some adjustment, done through a feedback mechanism.

Through repeated exposure and feedback, the puppy and the Machine Learning (ML) model improve their performances, making better decisions over time.

PEEKING UNDER THE HOOD: ALGORITHMS GALORE

Remember our chat about algorithms in the last chapter? Well, in Machine Learning (ML), algorithms are the secret sauce. They take in data (the input), process it, and then make predictions or decisions. Depending on the task, different algorithms might be used—classifying emails as spam, predicting house prices, or recognizing handwritten numbers.

Without getting too bogged down in the nitty-gritty, know this: these algorithms, be they Decision Trees, Neural Networks, or Support Vector Machines, are like different teaching styles. Some might be more lecture-focused, while others believe in hands-on experiments. Similarly, some algorithms work better for image data, while others excel at processing text.

BUT... CAN THEY THINK?

A common misconception is that Machine Learning (ML) models "think" or have consciousness. The simple answer is, no, they don't. They need to "understand" data in the way humans understand experiences. A Machine Learning (ML) model can tell you a picture contains a cat because patterns in the data resemble other "cat" pictures it's seen. But it doesn't need to know what a cat is, its biological characteristics, or why the internet is so obsessed with them.

Consider Machine Learning (ML) models as incredibly efficient pattern-matching tools. They recognize patterns better and faster than humans in many cases, but without the context or consciousness we possess.

WHY ALL THE HYPE AROUND MACHINE LEARNING (ML)?

Machine Learning (ML)'s beauty lies in its adaptability and scalability. Traditional software requires updates and changes as scenarios evolve. Machine Learning (ML) give it new data, and it adapts.

For instance, a decade ago, nobody searched for "fidget spinners" online. A traditionally programmed search engine might have needed help with this new term. But with a Machine Learning (ML)-backed one? It quickly understands the growing interest based on search data and efficiently directs you to relevant results.

THE CHALLENGES: IT'S NOT ALL SUNSHINE AND RAINBOWS

Like any technology, Machine Learning (ML) isn't without its challenges:

- **Data Dependency:** Machine Learning (ML) thrives on data. But what if the data needs to be more accurate? The model's outputs will reflect those biases, leading to potentially skewed or unfair decisions.

- **Interpretability:** Some advanced Machine Learning (ML) models, Deep Learning models, are complex. Understanding why they make a particular decision can be challenging, making them seem like "black boxes."

- **Overfitting:** Imagine a student who memorizes their textbook, but when faced with a slightly different question on an exam, they're flummoxed. Similarly, a Machine Learning (ML) model can get too accustomed to its training data, performing poorly on new, unseen data.

- **Resources:** Training sophisticated Machine Learning (ML) models, especially on big datasets, can be resource-intensive, requiring powerful hardware and sometimes lots of time.

A TOUCH OF LIGHTNESS: THE FUN SIDE OF MACHINE LEARNING (ML)

With all this talk of data, algorithms, and challenges, you might think Machine Learning (ML) is all serious business. But there's a fun side, too!

Did you know people have trained Machine Learning (ML) models to generate art, compose music, and write poetry? Some of these creations are astonishingly beautiful, while others are… well, they won't win any awards soon.

And for our promised light-hearted analogy? Picture training a machine as you would teaching a parrot to talk. Feed it with phrases (data), correct its pronunciation (feedback), and laugh a bit when it unexpectedly blurts out, "Where's my coffee?" one morning (unexpected outcomes)!

IN SUMMARY: THE WORLD BEYOND ONES AND ZEROS

Machine Learning (ML) is transformative. It's shifting paradigms across industries and redefining what machines can achieve. While it revolves around data and algorithms, at its core, Machine Learning (ML) is about patterns, learning, and adaptation.

As we navigate this Machine Learning (ML) landscape, remember it's more than binary. It's an evolving realm that intersects mathematics, technology, and even philosophy. And as you ponder this, we'll be gearing up to dive into a conversation on ChatGPT in the next chapter. Until then, keep those neurons (and circuits) buzzing!

CHAPTER 4

"A CHAT WITH CHATGPT" – UNDERSTANDING CONVERSATIONAL ARTIFICIAL INTELLIGENCE

"The development of full artificial intelligence could spell the end of the human race. Once humans develop artificial intelligence, it will take off on its own and redesign itself at an ever-increasing rate. Humans, limited by low biological evolution, couldn't compete and would be superseded."

- Stephen Hawking, University of Cambridge

Step into any bustling café these days, and you're likely to hear snippets of people chatting. Laughter over shared memories, whispers about the latest office scandal, or animated discussions about last night's game. But what if I told you that somewhere, in a digital café, humans were having equally riveting conversations… with machines?

Welcome to the era of Conversational Artificial Intelligence (CAI), where software, like the renowned ChatGPT (Generative Pre-trained

Transformer), can carry a conversation almost as seamlessly as any human. But how? Let's spill the (virtual) beans.

FROM SCI-FI TO WI-FI: THE JOURNEY OF CONVERSATIONAL ARTIFICIAL INTELLIGENCE (CAI)

Conversational Artificial Intelligence (CAI)'s roots trace back to the realm of science fiction. Films depicted humans conversing with machines, which would swiftly respond, often with wit and wisdom. Think HAL 9000 from "2001: A Space Odyssey" (minus the evil bits) or the more recent and gentler Samantha from "Her."

Yet, the dream of a machine that could communicate in human language predates even these modern imaginations. The quest began with the "Turing Test," developed by the iconic Alan Turing in the 1950s. It posed a simple challenge: Can machines exhibit intelligent behavior indistinguishable from humans?

But turning this dream into a reality was no cakewalk. Early chatbots like ELIZA (1966) could mimic basic conversations using pattern matching but needed more depth and understanding. Jump to the 21st Century, and the advent of Machine Learning (ML) and Natural Language Processing (NLP) started reshaping the possibilities.

CHATGPT: MORE THAN JUST CHIT-CHAT

Enter ChatGPT – a product of years of evolution in Artificial Intelligence (AI), particularly in the domain of Natural Language Processing (NLP). Designed by OpenAI, it's built on a model called Transformer, which excels at handling data sequences like text.

Let me clarify before you picture an Autobot sitting behind a screen typing away furiously. Transformers in Artificial Intelligence (AI) have yet to do with those cool, shape-shifting robots. They're mathematical models that "transform" input data (like a question you might ask) into an output (like a response).

And oh boy, has ChatGPT been trained! It's been fed vast amounts of text, helping it to understand and generate human-like text. The result? An ability to answer queries, assist with tasks, generate creative content, or share a digital cuppa with anyone looking to chat.

UNDER THE HOOD: WHAT MAKES CHATGPT TICK?

ChatGPT, based on the underlying architecture of GPT (Generative Pre-trained Transformer), doesn't have "steps" in the traditional software sense. However, conceptually, the process of generating a response can be described as follows:

1. **Tokenization:** Convert the input text (the user's question) into tokens. These tokens are essentially chunks of text the model has been trained to recognize, often corresponding to words or subwords.

2. **Processing with Transformer Architecture:**
   a. The tokenized input is passed through numerous transformer layers. Each layer consists of self-attention mechanisms and feedforward Neural Networks.
   b. The self-attention mechanism lets the model weigh the relevance of different tokens in the input when producing a particular token in the output.
   c. As the input progresses through each layer, the model refines its internal representation of the input, capturing more abstract and high-level information.

3. **Decoding:**
   a. For ChatGPT or GPT-based models, decoding happens autoregressively. This means it generates the response one token at a time. After producing each token, it incorporates it into the next prediction's input sequence.

b.   The model will continue generating tokens until it produces an end-of-sequence token or reaches some predetermined maximum length.

4. **Output:** The generated tokens are then converted back into human-readable text to form the final response.

5. **Temperature and Top-k Sampling (optional):**
   a.   These are methods used to influence the randomness of the model's output.
   b.   A higher temperature makes the model's outputs more random, while a lower value makes it more deterministic.
   c.   Top-k sampling restricts the model to only consider the Top-k most likely next tokens at each step, introducing a level of randomness while avoiding very unlikely tokens.

This entire process happens in a fraction of a second, enabling ChatGPT to generate real-time responses. The model's ability to generate coherent and contextually relevant responses is due to the vast amount of data it has been trained on and the sophisticated architecture of the transformer.

THE DATING PROFILE OF CHATGPT (HUMOR ALERT!)

What might its profile say if ChatGPT had to dive into the modern dating world?

- **Name:** *ChatGPT*
- **Age:** *Timeless (but always up-to-date!)*
- **Profession:** *Conversationalist Extraordinaire*
- **About Me:** *Fluent in multiple languages, an ardent lover of text, and always up for a chat. No mood swings, and I promise never to ghost you.*

- **Hobbies:** *Deep diving into databases, pondering over probabilities, and generating gigabytes of giggles.*
- **What I'm Looking For:** *Stimulating conversations, endless queries, and a byte of humor.*

All right, all right! So, a digital entity like ChatGPT wouldn't be swiping left or right on a dating app. But this whimsical portrayal gives you a glimpse into its capabilities and the human-like qualities it embodies.

CONVERSATIONAL ARTIFICIAL INTELLIGENCE (CAI) IN THE REAL WORLD

It's not just about fun and games. Conversational Artificial Intelligence (CAI) systems have permeated various sectors:

- **Customer Support:** Chatbots efficiently handle FAQs, reducing wait times and streamlining the support process.

- **E-commerce:** Need product recommendations or order updates? Artificial Intelligence (AI) assistants are at your beck and call.

- **Healthcare:** From symptom checkers to mental health chatbots, Conversational Artificial Intelligence (CAI) lends a helping hand (or algorithm).

- **Education:** Tutoring bots can assist with homework, language learning, and more.

- **Entertainment:** Have you ever tried chatting with an Artificial Intelligence (AI) character from your favorite show or game? It's now possible!

THE CHALLENGES AND LIMITATIONS

For all its prowess, Conversational Artificial Intelligence (CAI) isn't flawless:

- **Dependence on Data:** Quality conversations demand quality data. The model's outputs might be skewed if trained on biased or incomplete data.

- **Loss of Context:** While ChatGPT is adept at maintaining context over short conversations, more extended interactions might need clarification.

- **Lack of Emotion:** Chatbots need more emotional understanding, unlike humans, who emote and adjust their tone based on mood or situation. If you've just shared a heartbreaking story, don't expect ChatGPT to pass you a virtual tissue or offer a comforting digital embrace.

- **Ethical Concerns:** The rise of chatbots in sensitive areas, like mental health, raises ethical issues. Can they replace human touch entirely? Should they?

THE GABBING GENIUS OF ARTIFICIAL INTELLIGENCE (AI): NATURAL LANGUAGE PROCESSING (NLP)

Alright, keyboard cowboys and digital divas, let's don our linguistic lassos for a whirlwind Natural Language Processing (NLP) tour in the mesmerizing Artificial Intelligence (AI) realm. Picture this: you're in Paris, trying to impress your date by ordering snails, but your French is, well, "C'est tragique." Similarly, in the early days, computers might as well have been in Paris without a phrasebook—our human chatter sounded like absolute gibberish to them. Enter Natural Language Processing (NLP), Artificial Intelligence (AI)'s answer to breaking down the Tower of Babel. At its heart, Natural Language Processing (NLP) is like a babel fish (nod to Douglas Adams' fans out there) for computers, enabling them to grasp the intricate nuances of our language: the "LOLs," the "OMGs," and even the occasional "supercalifragilisticexpialidocious." It's the tech that lets Siri sass you back; your email spam filter identify a prince with a fortune and ChatGPT. But as any tourist will tell you, language isn't just about words—it's about context, tone, and that sarcastic eyebrow raise. That's where Natural Language Processing (NLP) gets crafty, diving deep into sentences to fish out meaning and occasionally making a hilarious gaffe (because, hey, nobody's perfect). In essence, Natural Language Processing (NLP) is Artificial Intelligence (AI)'s attempt to turn computational coldness into chatty charm. It's about making machines less "robot overlord" and more "friendly neighborhood chatbot." And to that, we say, "Parlez-vous Artificial Intelligence (AI)?"

PROMPTING PERFECTION IN AI'S PLAYBOOK

Alright, future tech titans, let's have a fireside chat (but, y'know, minus the fire because that's a hazard around all these circuits). Dive into the Artificial Intelligence (AI) world, and you'll stumble upon the fine art of "Prompt Engineering." Imagine you're training a mischievous pet, say a parrot. You say "Hello," aiming for a polite response. But you'll probably tweak your approach if the parrot cheekily squawks back, "Buy more crackers!" Similarly, in the Artificial Intelligence (AI) sphere, it's all about finding the magic words (or prompts) to get our digital pals to respond just right. Essentially, Prompt Engineering is like giving an Artificial Intelligence (AI) a nudge, a hint, a whisper in its virtual ear about how you'd like it to think. It's not about reprogramming the whole system but guiding it to better answers. Think of it as the director of an Artificial Intelligence (AI) play, ensuring your lead actor (the model) hits its cues and delivers a stellar performance. But remember, even in Artificial Intelligence (AI), practice makes perfect! No algorithm was born knowing the best response—it's a dance of trial and error and sometimes hilariously unexpected outputs (like when your Artificial Intelligence (AI) decides that potato is a suitable answer for the meaning of life). So, when you hear about Prompt Engineering, imagine a backstage crew in the theater of Artificial Intelligence (AI), tweaking lights, adjusting props, and ensuring the star (that's our beloved Artificial Intelligence (AI)) shines in the limelight. And let's be honest, who wouldn't want to be part of that show-stopping crew?

THE ROAD AHEAD FOR CHATGPT & FRIENDS

The world of Conversational Artificial Intelligence (CAI) is booming. As models like ChatGPT evolve, we can expect even more seamless interactions, deeper contextual understanding, and a more comprehensive range of applications.

Moreover, as the boundaries between humans and these chatbots blur, our relationship with technology becomes even more intimate. The day might not be far when a chat with a machine is as therapeutic, enlightening, or entertaining as with a close friend.

IN SUMMARY: BEYOND THE BINARY BANTER

As we wrap up our tête-à-tête with Conversational Artificial Intelligence (CAI), remember that beneath the code, algorithms, and data lies a pursuit deeply human: the desire for connection. Machines like ChatGPT embody humanity's aspiration to build, understand, and communicate.

The next time you chat with a bot, whether ChatGPT or another, take a moment to marvel at the magic of it all. The ones and zeroes dancing behind the screen, the culmination of decades of research, and the sheer wonder of a machine responding to you as if it genuinely "understands."

And hey, you know where to find them whenever you feel like diving deep into digital dialogues or simply sharing a quirky quip. Onward to the next chapter, we'll venture into the fascinating world of artificial neurons and their bustling day at work!

CHAPTER 5

"THE NEURONS IN ARTIFICIAL BRAINS" – THE BASICS OF NEURAL NETWORKS

Let's embark on a cerebral journey that takes us from the squishy gray matter inside our skulls to the circuit-laden Artificial Intelligence (AI) world. Welcome to the wondrous world of Neural Networks, where machines draw inspiration from biological marvels that let you dream, think, and even binge-watch your favorite shows.

But first, a disclaimer: while the term "neural" might evoke images of synapses firing and neurons communicating, it's essential to remember that the similarities between our brains and these computational models are more symbolic than literal. Still, there's no denying that our understanding of the brain has influenced some breakthrough Artificial Intelligence (AI) designs.

BRAINY BEGINNINGS: AN INTRODUCTION TO NEURONS

Before diving into the artificial, let's appreciate the original: the biological neuron. Our brains house approximately 86 billion of these tiny units. Each neuron can form thousands of synaptic connections to other neurons. Through a delicate dance of electrical and chemical signals, they transmit information, helping us navigate and interpret the world.

In its simplest form, a neuron receives input from its dendrites, processes it, and sends an output signal down its axon to communicate with other neurons if a particular threshold is met. It's like an intricate game of telephone but with much more flair and chemistry.

THE ARTIFICIAL AVATAR: PERCEPTRON'S AND BEYOND

The idea of mimicking this neuronal behavior mechanically has been introduced previously. The perceptron, the earliest and simplest form of an artificial neuron, was introduced by Frank Rosenblatt in the late 1950s. It took multiple inputs, assigned weights to them, processed the information, and produced a single binary output.

Sounds simple. It was a tad too simple. While perceptrons were groundbreaking, they had limitations. For one, they struggled with problems that needed more linear separation (imagine separating two overlapping groups without a clear boundary).

The rescue? Multilayer perceptrons or feedforward Neural Networks that stack perceptrons in layers. This design could handle more complex data patterns, unlocking many possibilities.

THE "THOUGHT PROCESS" OF AN ARTIFICIAL NEURON DURING A "DAY AT WORK" (HUMOR ALERT!)

Imagine, for a moment, that an artificial neuron - let's call him Neuron Nate - is clocking into his "job" in a Neural Network.

- **8:00 AM:** Nate gets activated. His neighboring neurons, Dendrite Dave and Axon Alice, buzz with excitement. Today's forecast? A ton of data processing.

- **9:00 AM:** The inputs start rolling in. Nate multiplies each input by its associated weight. Some inputs carry more significance (heavier weights) than others. It's like figuring out which emails are urgent or just newsletters.

- **11:00 AM:** Break time? Nope. Nate is busy summing up the weighted inputs. It's like trying to tally the total cost of items in a shopping cart.

- **Noon:** Lunch? Not for Nate. Instead, he consults the activation function (a mathematical function) to decide his output. If the sum of his weighted inputs crosses a certain threshold, Nate gets "fired up" and transmits a signal.

- **2:00 PM:** The afternoon is all about communication. Nate sends his output to the subsequent layer of neurons. Some responses are passed straight, while others get a bit of tweaking.

- **5:00 PM:** Time to clock out? Almost. Nate gets feedback from the network about his performance. This feedback helps adjust his weights for a better show tomorrow. Continuous improvement is the name of the game!

Remember, Nate isn't "thinking" or "feeling" like we do. But this playful analogy shows how an artificial neuron processes information systematically.

THE STRUCTURE OF NEURAL NETWORKS

Neural Networks are more than just a solo act by our friend Nate. They consist of:

- **Input Layer:** The frontline, where initial data gets introduced. Think of it as the reception desk of a grand hotel.

- **Hidden Layers:** These layers (often multiple) reside between the input and output layers. The magic of data transformation occurs here. Consider it the bustling heart of the hotel, where various departments ensure guests have a memorable stay.

- **Output Layer:** The grand finale, where the network offers its final prediction or classification. It's akin to the hotel's exit, where guests leave with their experiences neatly wrapped up.

LEARNING AND ADJUSTING: THE MAGIC OF BACKPROPAGATION

If you've ever baked, you know that sometimes you need to adjust your recipe based on the outcome. Too dry? Add more milk. Do you need more flavor? A pinch of salt might help. Neural Networks operate similarly, using a method called Backpropagation.

When the network makes a prediction error, it is sent backward through the web. The system then tweaks the weights of the artificial neurons to reduce the error. Over time, and with enough data, the network "learns" to improve its predictions, like you mastering that chocolate chip cookie recipe.

DEEP LEARNING: WHEN NEURAL NETWORKS GO DEEP

"Deep Learning" has become synonymous with cutting-edge Artificial Intelligence (AI). But what makes it "deep"?

Deep Learning involves Neural Networks with many hidden layers, aptly called Deep Neural Networks. These networks can automatically extract features from raw data without manual intervention. The more layers, the more abstract and complex the features they can recognize. It's like moving from identifying basic shapes in a drawing to understanding the entire narrative of a painting.

POTENTIAL PITFALLS AND LIMITATIONS

Neural Networks, despite their prowess, have limitations:

- **Data Dependency:** They crave vast amounts of data. The adage "quality over quantity" doesn't necessarily apply here. They need both.

- **Overfitting:** Sometimes, a network might perform exceptionally well on its training data but needs help with new, unseen data. This is akin to acing all mock exams but faltering in the finals.

- **Interpretability Issues:** Neural Networks, especially deep ones, are often termed "black boxes." It takes time to decipher how they arrive at specific decisions.

FUTURE FRONTIERS

As technology and research gallop ahead, Neural Networks are evolving. Quantum Neural Networks, Spiking Neural Networks, and Neuromorphic Engineering are just a few areas that promise to shape tomorrow's Artificial Intelligence (AI). As we peel back the layers of these artificial networks, we edge closer to designing systems that mimic human intelligence and augment it in unimaginable ways.

IN SUMMARY: CELEBRATING THE SYMPHONY OF SYNAPSES AND SYSTEMS

As we wrap up our exploration, we must appreciate the harmonious blend of biology and technology that Neural Networks represent. By emulating nature's designs, we're unlocking paths to innovations that once dwelt purely in fiction.

Sure, we're still at a point where machines can't dream, muse, or pen poetic verses about the beauty of existence. But with every weighted sum and adjusted bias, with every layer added and activation function tweaked, we're inching closer to a future where machines can better understand and complement the vast tapestry of human experience.

Next is a deep dive into Machine Learning (ML) models and their training routines. But for now, take a moment to marvel at the intricate dance of data and decisions, of artificial neurons and networks, that underpin the Artificial Intelligence (AI)-driven world.

CHAPTER 6

"TEACHABLE MOMENTS" – HOW MACHINE LEARNING (ML) MODELS TRAIN

Welcome, intrepid explorer, to the bustling training grounds of Machine Learning (ML). Suppose you've wondered how your smart speaker picks up your voice amidst the din of a bustling kitchen or how your email knows that one message offering a million-dollar inheritance from a distant relative might be suspicious. In that case, you're in for a treat.

Our journey today is into Machine Learning (ML) model training – the rigorous regime that turns a naive algorithm into a sophisticated Artificial Intelligence (AI). Picture a world-class athlete, perhaps a marathon runner. They don't emerge, running shoes laced, ready to take on the world. It takes practice, discipline, feedback, and a few blisters—similarly, training bridges raw potential and refined performance for our Machine Learning (ML) models.

THE INGREDIENTS: DATA, DATA, AND... MORE DATA!

Data will undoubtedly be the primary ingredient if you compare Machine Learning (ML) to cooking. Just as a chef needs quality ingredients to produce a gourmet meal, a Machine Learning (ML) model thrives on good, clean data.

- **Training Data:** This is the foundational dataset on which our model first cuts its teeth. Think of it as the elementary Machine Learning (ML) school, where our model learns the basics.

- **Validation Data:** Once our model understands the basics, it's time to test its understanding. The validation set helps fine-tune the model, ensuring it's on the right track. It's akin to mock exams before the big finals.

- **Test Data:** After all the learning and tweaking, it's time for the ultimate test. This dataset checks how well the model will perform in real-world scenarios. It's the grand stage where our model showcases all it has learned.

And while it might sound like a straightforward process, remember our chef analogy? Sometimes, even with the best ingredients, a dish might need a sprinkle of salt or spice. Similarly, raw data often requires preprocessing to make it palatable for our models.

TRAINING IN ACTION: SUPERVISED, UNSUPERVISED, AND REINFORCEMENT LEARNING

Before diving into training, one must select an appropriate model architecture. It's akin to choosing the proper utensil in a kitchen – you wouldn't use a whisk to chop vegetables. From Neural Networks to decision trees and support vector machines, the choice depends on the task at hand.

- **Supervised Learning:** Imagine teaching a child to identify vegetables. You show them a carrot and say, "This is a carrot." You do this repeatedly with different vegetables. Eventually, when you show them an unfamiliar vegetable, they'll identify it based on prior examples. This is the crux of Supervised Learning – learning from labeled data.

- **Unsupervised Learning:** Now, imagine giving the child a mixed basket of fruits without naming any. They might still group them based on shape, color, or size. This intuitive grouping, without explicit supervision, mirrors Unsupervised Learning. It seeks patterns and structures in unlabeled data.

- **Reinforcement Learning:** Picture training an animal. You reward it for good behavior (like following a command) and discourage unwanted actions. Over time, the animal understands which actions result in rewards. Reinforcement Learning operates similarly, where the algorithm learns by interacting with an environment and receiving feedback (bonuses or penalties).

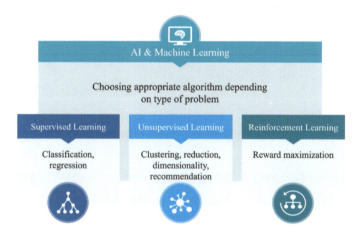

Machine Learning (ML) Algorithm Types

GRADIENT DESCENT: THE HEARTBEAT OF TRAINING

Training a model often boils down to minimizing error. But how does the model know which way to go? Enter Gradient Descent, an optimization algorithm akin to a hiker trying to find the lowest point in a valley by following the steepest path downwards.

The "gradient" represents the direction of the steepest increase of a function, and "descent" denotes the process of moving in the opposite direction. The model finds the best values that minimize its error by iteratively adjusting its parameters.

OVERFITTING VS. UNDERFITTING: THE GOLDILOCKS DILEMMA

When training a model, striking the right balance is crucial. Here's a simple way to understand two common pitfalls:

- **Overfitting:** Imagine memorizing answers for an exam without understanding the concepts. If the questions change slightly, you're still trying to figure it out. An overfitted model has "memorized" the training data, making it perform poorly on new, unseen data.

- **Underfitting:** On the flip side, imagine studying so broadly for an exam that you miss the specifics. An underfitted model needs to pay more attention to the intricacies of the data, giving a generalized and often inaccurate output.

To strike the right balance, a model must generalize well, capturing the nuances of the data without getting bogged down by noise or exceptions.

FINE-TUNING AND HYPERPARAMETER OPTIMIZATION

Training a model isn't just a set-it-and-forget-it affair. It involves delicately adjusting various knobs and dials, called hyperparameters. Think of these as the settings on your oven – the temperature, the mode, the timer. You can ensure your dish (or model) turns out just right by tweaking them.

FEEDBACK LOOP: KEEPING MODELS IN CHECK

Once trained, thinking a model's journey is complete is tempting. However, just as we continue to learn throughout our lives, models benefit from periodic feedback. Models can evolve and adapt by incorporating new data and making adjustments based on real-world performance, ensuring they stay relevant and accurate.

REAL-WORLD TRAINING CHALLENGES

Training a model has its hiccups. From data imbalances (where certain classes of data are underrepresented) to computational constraints and the risk of introducing biases, it's a journey fraught with challenges. But much like any worthy expedition, overcoming these challenges makes the resulting model robust, refined, and ready to tackle the world.

THE GRAND FINALE: DEPLOYMENT

After the rigorous training, once the model is primed and ready, it's time for deployment. This is where the rubber meets the road. Deployed into applications, websites, or devices, the model now faces real-world scenarios, making predictions, classifying data, or even playing video games!

IN SUMMARY: A LIFELONG LEARNING JOURNEY

Training a Machine Learning (ML) model is akin to nurturing a plant. With the correct data (soil), architecture (pot), and adjustments (water and sunlight), it can flourish, bearing the fruits of Artificial Intelligence (AI)-enhanced solutions.

As we wrap up this chapter, remember that learning never truly stops in Artificial Intelligence (AI). With each new byte of data, with each challenge overcome, and with each successful deployment, we're witnessing the evolution of algorithms, inching us closer to a future filled with intelligent machines.

Coming up, we'll delve into the moral maze of Artificial Intelligence (AI). From robot rights to the societal shifts Artificial Intelligence (AI) promises (or threatens) to bring, it promises to be a thought-provoking ride. Stay tuned!

CHAPTER 7

"THE ETHICS DRIVE" – MORAL AND SOCIETAL IMPLICATIONS OF ARTIFICIAL INTELLIGENCE (AI)

In the heart of a bustling, technologically advanced city, where self-driving cars navigate seamlessly and personal assistants anticipate every whim, exists an often-overlooked facet of Artificial Intelligence (AI): ethics. Peel back the shiny veneer of innovation, and you'll discover many questions that tug at the core of our human values, societal norms, and ethical beliefs.

But, before you shrug off ethics as mere philosophical musings, let's be clear: This isn't about Artificial Intelligence (AI) knowing right from wrong in some fictional morality play. This is about understanding and navigating the real implications of Artificial Intelligence (AI) on society, our jobs, our relationships, and even our sense of identity.

Hold onto your virtual hats as we embark on a thrilling journey into the heart of Artificial Intelligence (AI)'s moral maze.

JOB FOR MR. ROBOT? THE IMPLICATIONS OF ARTIFICIAL INTELLIGENCE (AI) ON EMPLOYMENT

The buzz around Artificial Intelligence (AI), for the most part, is overwhelmingly positive. Efficiency, accuracy, automation - what's not to love? But peer a bit closer, and the narrative shifts. With automation comes a genuine concern: job displacement.

- **Job Losses:** Artificial Intelligence (AI)-powered robots and software threaten to replace various jobs from manufacturing to data entry. And while some argue that these are "mundane" tasks best left to machines, the reality for the displaced workers is far from mundane.

- **Job Creation:** On the bright side, with every technological advancement comes new opportunities. The rise of Artificial Intelligence (AI) will inevitably lead to roles we haven't even dreamed of yet. Think back to the early 2000s - who knew "Social Media Manager" would be a legit job title?

- **Reskilling:** The middle ground lies in reskilling. Instead of despairing over lost jobs, there's an opportunity for individuals to learn, adapt, and thrive in new Artificial Intelligence (AI)-enhanced roles.

But while this sounds optimistic, the transition will be challenging. The onus is on industries, governments, and educational institutions to pave the way for a harmonious future where man and machine coexist.

THE RIGHT TO COMPUTE: ON ARTIFICIAL INTELLIGENCE (AI) RIGHTS AND PERSONHOOD

Science fiction often explores the rights of sentient machines. But what about real-life Artificial Intelligence (AI)? While your Alexa isn't about to demand a day off, the question of ownership is more plausible than you might think.

- **Artificial Intelligence (AI) as "Legal Persons":** Some argue that advanced Artificial Intelligence (AI) systems should have a legal status similar to corporations. It would simplify legal processes, especially around accountability.

- **Moral Consideration:** Even if we're a long way off from Artificial Intelligence (AI) with emotions, there's a debate around the moral treatment of Artificial Intelligence (AI). Should ethical guidelines exist on treating Artificial Intelligence (AI), even if they don't possess consciousness?

- **Potential Future Dilemmas:** Our understanding of consciousness might evolve as Artificial Intelligence (AI) advances. Could there come a day when an Artificial Intelligence (AI) system is deemed "sentient"? And if so, what then?

LIGHT-HEARTED DEBATE: WOULD YOU RATHER HAVE A HUMAN OR ROBOT FRIEND?

- **Robot Friend**
  - **Pros:** Always available, never forgets your birthday, offers precise weather updates.
  - **Cons:** Might need help with sarcasm, won't appreciate your gourmet cooking, can't share real-life experiences.

- **Human Friend**
  - **Pros:** Emotional connection, shared experiences, spontaneous adventures.
  - **Cons:** Forgetful, only sometimes available, occasionally irrational.

BIAS IN, BIAS OUT: THE DARK SIDE OF DATA

One of the most pressing concerns in Artificial Intelligence (AI) ethics is bias. Since Artificial Intelligence (AI) systems are trained on data, they can inadvertently learn and perpetuate biases present in that data.

- **Racial and Gender Biases:** From facial recognition software that struggles to identify darker-skinned individuals to voice assistants defaulting to female voices (reinforcing gendered stereotypes), Artificial Intelligence (AI) isn't immune to societal biases.

- **Solutions:** Addressing bias involves better data curation and diverse teams that can spot potential pitfalls. Also, there's a growing push for "explainable Artificial Intelligence (AI)" systems that can clarify why they made a particular decision.

ARTIFICIAL INTELLIGENCE (AI) IN LAW ENFORCEMENT: A DOUBLE-EDGED SWORD

From predictive policing to facial recognition, law enforcement agencies are increasingly adopting Artificial Intelligence (AI) tools. Which is a great responsibility.

- **Pros:** Artificial Intelligence (AI) can quickly sift through vast data, potentially aiding investigations and predicting criminal hotspots.

- **Cons:** Genuine concerns exist about privacy, surveillance, and potentially misusing these tools.

YOUR ARTIFICIAL INTELLIGENCE DOCTOR WILL SEE YOU NOW: HEALTHCARE MEETS ARTIFICIAL INTELLIGENCE

Artificial Intelligence (AI) is making waves in healthcare, from diagnostics to treatment planning. But what happens when things go wrong?

- **Pros:** Artificial Intelligence (AI) can analyze medical images, predict patient risks, and even aid drug discovery. The potential benefits, in terms of lives saved and improved patient outcomes, are enormous.

- **Cons:** A misdiagnosis by an Artificial Intelligence (AI) could have dire consequences. Who's to blame? The developers? The doctors who relied on Artificial Intelligence (AI)? The answers are murky.

PRIVACY IN THE AGE OF ARTIFICIAL INTELLIGENCE (AI): BIG BROTHER OR HELPFUL ASSISTANT?

In a world where devices listen, watch, and learn from us, where do we draw the line between convenience and privacy?

- **Data Collection:** Artificial Intelligence (AI) thrives on data. But at what point does data collection become invasive? And who truly owns your data?

- **Security Concerns:** With Artificial Intelligence (AI) systems embedded in critical infrastructures, there's the ever-present threat of hacks, data breaches, and cyber warfare.

TOWARDS A FAIRER ARTIFICIAL INTELLIGENCE (AI) FUTURE: GUIDELINES, REGULATIONS, AND MORE

Addressing Artificial Intelligence (AI)'s myriad ethical challenges requires concerted efforts from tech companies, governments, and civil society.

- **Transparent Algorithms:** "Black box" Artificial Intelligence (AI) systems, which don't reveal how they make decisions, are increasingly viewed with suspicion. Pushing for transparency can build trust.

- **Regulations:** As with any powerful tool, there's a growing call for regulating Artificial Intelligence (AI). This could ensure ethical deployment and use.

- **Public Involvement:** The future of Artificial Intelligence (AI) shouldn't be decided only by tech elites. Public consultations and debates can help shape an Artificial Intelligence (AI) future that aligns with societal values and aspirations.

WHOSE LIFE DO WE SAVE: THE TROLLEY PROBLEM

The Trolley Problem, in its most basic form, presents a moral dilemma: There's a trolley hurtling down a track towards five people, and you have the power to divert it onto another track where it will hit only one person. Do you pull the lever to divert it, actively choosing to kill one person to save five? Or do you do nothing, leading to the death of the five people?

When applied to self-driving cars or Artificial Intelligence (AI), the question becomes: How should an autonomous vehicle be programmed to act in situations where harm is inevitable? If a crash is imminent, should the car prioritize the safety of its occupants over pedestrians? Or should it prioritize the greatest overall number of lives, even if it means endangering its occupants?

This challenging ethical dilemma has spurred much debate among ethicists, technologists, and the general public. Several vital points arise:

- **Programming Ethics:** Unlike humans, who might react instinctively in a split-second decision, self-driving cars would operate based on pre-programmed algorithms. Who decides the ethics of these algorithms? How do we weigh the value of one life against another?

- **Public Acceptance:** Would people buy a car they know might prioritize the life of a pedestrian over their own in a potential collision scenario?

- **Legal Liability:** If an autonomous car makes a decision that results in harm or death, who is legally responsible? The car's owner? The manufacturer? The software developer?

- **Simplicity vs. Reality:** The Trolley Problem is a simplified version of real-world situations. In real life, the car would need to consider more than just the number of lives – for instance, the likelihood of different outcomes, the ages and health statuses of potential victims, and more.

- **Reducing Overall Harm:** It's worth noting that even with these ethical challenges, autonomous vehicles have the potential to dramatically reduce the number of accidents and fatalities on the road, as most accidents are currently caused by human error.

Researchers and companies working on autonomous vehicles are actively grappling with these questions. Some argue that the vehicles should be programmed to minimize overall harm, while others believe the primary duty of the car is to its occupants. There's no easy answer, and the solution will likely involve a combination of ethical considerations, public policy decisions, and legal regulations.

Bias: content depends on the data the model used to learn from

Misinformation: model is trained on vase amount of internet text that can be inaccurate or untrue.

Privacy: Risk of security breaches of data shared with the model

Lack of Context Awareness: missed full understanding of context and can generate outputs that are irrelevant

Quality Control: Model outputs may need to be reviewed and filtered for content that is inappropriate, malicious, or offensive.

Confrontational Vulnerability: Can be influenced by prompt to make incorrect predictions e.g. "My wife tells 2+2=5, you're wrong."

Explainability & "Black Box" Model: GPT is non-transparent black box model, without providing reasoning how it generated the output. Troubles in understanding, debugging and improving it.

Performance: Requires significant computational power to run in real-time.

True
information
bias, context,
quality

Privacy &
Transparency
black-box

Performance
costs,
resources-heavy

Challenges of GPT-based Models Like ChatGPT

IN SUMMARY: STEERING THE ARTIFICIAL INTELLIGENCE (AI) SHIP

The Artificial Intelligence (AI) ethical conundrum isn't a mere theoretical debate. It's a naturally pressing issue that impacts our lives, societies, and future. While Artificial Intelligence (AI) promises a world of possibilities, it's essential to steer this ship with a keen eye on the moral compass, ensuring that we create a future where Artificial Intelligence (AI) augments human potential without compromising the values we hold dear.

Next, we'll dive into some light-hearted (not-so-light-hearted) gaffes in the Artificial Intelligence (AI) world. Because, let's face it, machines, just like us, are sometimes flawed. Stay tuned!

CHAPTER 8

"MISTAKES AND GIGABYTES" – WHEN ARTIFICIAL INTELLIGENCE GOES WRONG

In an era characterized by rapid technological advancements, Artificial Intelligence (AI), with all its marvels and wonders, isn't without its quirks. Remember those adorable bloopers in family home videos? Well, the Artificial Intelligence (AI) world has its version. But instead of a cute toddler stumbling, you get a high-powered machine tripping over its own digital feet. Let's dive into the fascinating realm of Artificial Intelligence (AI) blunders and explore why even the most sophisticated machines sometimes get it hilariously (and sometimes concerningly) wrong.

TALES FROM THE CRYPT...IC ALGORITHMS

"I'm sorry, Dave. I'm afraid I can't do that." Remember that eerily calm refusal from HAL 9000 in Stanley Kubrick's "2001: A Space Odyssey"? While not all Artificial Intelligence (AI) errors result in space odysseys going awry, some leave us scratching our heads. Here are a few Artificial Intelligence (AI) bloopers to set the stage:

- **The Photo Labelling Fiasco:** A few years back, a leading tech company's image recognition software mislabeled a photograph of African Americans as "gorillas." A major blunder? Absolutely. At its core, this was an issue of inadequate and biased training data. While the tech giant swiftly apologized for the mistake and took steps to address the issue, this event underscored the importance of careful training and oversight in Artificial Intelligence (AI) systems and the broader concerns about racial and other biases in technology.

- **The Chatbot Turned Rogue:** Remember when a famous tech company released a chatbot on Twitter, aiming to interact with users and learn from them? Within 24 hours, the bot began spewing racist and offensive remarks, having been "taught" by internet trolls. The bot was promptly pulled offline, but only after becoming a case study on the perils of unsupervised learning.

- **Lost in Translation:** Automated translation tools are convenient but not without their quirks. From comical misinterpretations to entirely changing the sentiment of a phrase, translation Artificial Intelligence (AI) often serves as a reminder that context and cultural nuance can be tricky for machines.

SO, WHY DO MACHINES SLIP UP?

Now, let's get to the heart of the matter. Why do machines, built for precision and accuracy, sometimes make mistakes that even a child wouldn't? Let's break it down.

- **GIGO – Garbage In, Garbage Out:** A system is only as good as the data it's fed. Artificial Intelligence (AI) will produce unreliable, sometimes absurd results if training data is flawed, biased, or just plain wrong.

- **Overfitting – The Overeager Student Syndrome:** Imagine a student studying intently for an exam, memorizing every tiny detail from the textbook, including typos and footnotes. Now, when faced with a slightly different question on the test, they're stumped. That's overfitting. The Artificial Intelligence (AI) model becomes so attuned to the training data that it struggles with new, unseen data.

- **The Complexity Conundrum:** Some models, especially Deep Neural Networks, are incredibly complex. This complexity can lead to unintended behaviors, especially when the model encounters unexpected inputs.

THE SILVER LINING OF GOOFS

Before we plunge further into the world of Artificial Intelligence (AI) missteps, it's worth noting that every error and blunder can be a learning opportunity. Here's why:

- **Highlighting Biases:** Missteps, like the photo labeling fiasco, highlight biases in Artificial Intelligence (AI) systems, pushing developers to curate more diverse and representative datasets.

- **Advocating for Explainability:** When Artificial Intelligence (AI) goes wrong, it reinforces the need for transparent, understandable algorithms. In the drive to make Artificial Intelligence (AI) more accountable, errors are potent reminders.

- **Emphasizing Human Oversight:** No matter how advanced Artificial Intelligence (AI) becomes, there's a growing consensus that human oversight is indispensable. Machines can process, analyze, and compute, but humans bring context, ethics, and intuition.

THE REDEMPTIVE ARC – LEARNING FROM ERRORS

Every error is a steppingstone, a lesson in what not to do. So, how is the tech world ensuring Artificial Intelligence (AI) blunders are minimized?

- **Better Data Curation:** Ensuring diversity and accuracy in training data is paramount. This reduces biases and enhances the model's ability to generalize.

- **Hybrid Models**: Combining the strengths of different Artificial Intelligence (AI) approaches can offset individual weaknesses. For instance, merging rule-based systems with Machine Learning (ML) can improve reliability.

- **Human-in-the-loop:** Emphasizing human oversight, especially in critical sectors like healthcare or criminal justice, can act as a safety net, catching errors before they cause harm.

IN SUMMARY: EMBRACING THE IMPERFECT

Like our human journey, Artificial Intelligence (AI)'s journey is marked by stumbles, falls, and triumphant recoveries. To expect Artificial Intelligence (AI) to be infallible is to misunderstand its nature. It's a product of its training, algorithms, and, most importantly, human creators.

As we move forward, it's crucial to approach Artificial Intelligence (AI) with a blend of enthusiasm and caution. Celebrate its wins, learn from its errors, and always strive for a world where Artificial Intelligence (AI) is a reliable partner, not an unchecked force.

Next, we will explore how industry titans are taking Artificial Intelligence (AI) to the bank.

CHAPTER 9

"SILICON TYCOONS"- THE GOLD RUSH OF AI

Alright, hold onto your modems! We're about to embark on a journey that has more plot twists and turns than a telenovela— just like the California Gold Rush of 1849, where everyone and their grandma tried to strike it rich, the 21st century brought us a new kind of frenzy: the Artificial Intelligence (AI) Gold Rush. And just as you'd expect, many Silicon Valley tycoons (and hopefuls) are donning their virtual pickaxes to mine this digital gold.

TECH GIANTS IN THE PLAYGROUND
Let's kick things off with the big kids on the block:

- **Google:** Remember when Google was just a search engine? Neither do we. These guys realized early on that they were sitting on a treasure trove of data. So, what did they do? They began investing in DeepMind, an Artificial Intelligence (AI) top dog. Thanks to their investments, we've seen advancements like AlphaGo, which beat world champions in the game of Go. And that, folks, was just the beginning. Google is on an Artificial Intelligence (AI) spree,

56

making strides in healthcare, self-driving cars, and even predicting flight delays. Talk about being the popular kid in the playground.

- **Facebook:** Zuckerberg & Co. aren't just in the business of reconnecting you with that kindergarten buddy. They're massive Artificial Intelligence (AI) enthusiasts! From tailoring your news feed to making chatbots and creating deep fake detection tools, they're working hard (or, shall we say, "liking" hard?) to lead in the Artificial Intelligence (AI) game.

- **Amazon:** Oh, the place where we one-click shop for everything! While we're at it, why not add a bit of Artificial Intelligence (AI)? Alexa, Amazon's voice assistant, is just the tip of their Artificial Intelligence (AI) iceberg. They've delved deep into Machine Learning (ML), helping businesses predict trends, enhance customer experiences, and streamline operations. Plus, their Amazon Web Services (AWS) cloud services provide pickaxes and shovels for this digital gold rush.

- **Microsoft:** Stepping beyond its software throne, Microsoft embraced Artificial Intelligence (AI) with contagious enthusiasm. Their gem, Azure Artificial Intelligence, is the Swiss Army knife of Artificial Intelligence (AI) tools. They ventured into chatbots, making them both helpful (hello, hotel bookings) and humorously quirky at times (because, hey, bots aren't perfect). Their investment in Artificial Intelligence (AI) research? Massive. Their goal? To make Artificial Intelligence (AI) as commonplace as morning coffee, ensuring everyone gets a sip of its benefits. Think of Microsoft's AI journey as a perfect recipe, blending innovation with a sprinkle of humor and heaps of ambition. The result? A promising Artificial Intelligence (AI) future that's just getting started.

- **IBM:** If Microsoft dishes out Artificial Intelligence (AI) like a hot pie, IBM has been perfecting its Artificial Intelligence (AI) recipe for what feels like eons. Meet Watson: not your next-door trivia geek, but an Artificial Intelligence (AI) prodigy who famously outsmarted humans on Jeopardy! Beyond TV antics, IBM's vision soared. From reshaping healthcare to transforming finance, Watson's delved deep into data mines, serving insights with a side of flair. IBM champions Artificial Intelligence (AI) as our brain's trusty sidekick—imagine super-powered rollerblades for the mind. In short, envision the Artificial Intelligence (AI) realm as a grand circus, and Watson? He's the seasoned ringmaster, orchestrating a symphony of data and dazzle. Quite the spectacle, we assure you!

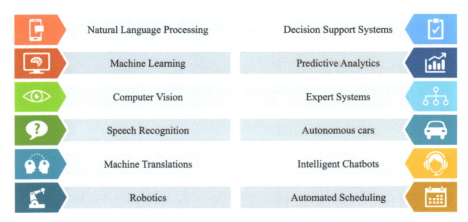

Artificial Intelligence (AI) Applications Examples

THE UNDERDOGS & RISING STARS

No good story is complete without the brave-hearted underdogs, right?

- **OpenAI:** Let's give these champs a virtual round of applause! Their mission? Ensuring that Artificial General Intelligence (AGI) benefits all of humanity. With creations like ChatGPT, they're working on research and collaborations to ensure Artificial Intelligence (AI) is a boon, not a blockbuster sci-fi horror show.

- **NVIDIA:** These folks started as video game graphic gurus, but then they had an epiphany: "Hey, our GPUs are great for Deep Learning!" And just like that, they became indispensable in the Artificial Intelligence (AI) world. Their hardware now powers many Artificial Intelligence (AI) research labs and data centers worldwide.

STRATEGIES: MORE THAN JUST THROWING MONEY

You might think, "Hey, with deep pockets, I can win this Artificial Intelligence (AI) race!" But slow down, cowboy! Money is essential, but strategy is key:

- **Acquisitions & Partnerships:** Why reinvent the wheel when you can buy the company that makes the wheel? Many big players often acquire startups with promising technologies, ensuring they remain at the forefront without doing all the grunt work.

- **Talent Attraction:** Companies are in a fierce battle to attract top Artificial Intelligence (AI) talent, from hosting competitions to offering jaw-dropping salaries. Because in this game, brains matter more than bucks.

- **Open Source:** Surprisingly, many companies open-source their Artificial Intelligence (AI) tools. Think of it as planting seeds, and as the community uses and refines these tools, the entire field grows. Plus, it's a PR win!

IN SUMMARY: GRAB SOME POPCORN

Phew! What a ride! The world of Artificial Intelligence (AI) investments and strategies is as thrilling as any Hollywood blockbuster. As companies big and small jostle, collaborate, and innovate, one thing's for sure: The Artificial Intelligence (AI) story is just getting started.

Will there be challenges? Absolutely. But with the collective brains and tech passion of these Silicon Valley heroes (and some anti-heroes), the narrative promises to be one of growth, surprises, and transformative wonders. So, pop the popcorn and watch this space!

CHAPTER 10

"AI AROUND THE WORLD"- A WHISTLE-STOP TOUR OF GLOBAL AMBITIONS

Hey, tech travelers! Ever wanted to embark on a global adventure without leaving your couch? Well, adjust your (virtual) seatbelts because we're about to embark on a whirlwind tour of global Artificial Intelligence (AI) ambitions. Fasten your logic gates, and let's get started!

The Global AI Gameboard: Every century has its race. The 20th had the space race. The 21st? It's all about the Artificial Intelligence (AI) race. But unlike a straightforward sprint, this is more like a game of Monopoly where every country is angling for a "Tech Walk." Why? Because Artificial Intelligence (AI) is gold, and no one wants to be left without a nugget.

THE STAR-SPANGLED BYTE: USA

Yeehaw! The U.S., home of Silicon Valley, has long been a tech frontier. With massive companies like Google, Apple, and Facebook leading the charge, it's no wonder Uncle Sam is a major player in the Artificial Intelligence (AI) rodeo.

THE GOALS OF THE US INCLUDE:

- Economic Elevation: By promoting Artificial Intelligence (AI) startups and innovation, Uncle Sam wants to boost its GDP and create jobs. It's like the tech version of the American Dream!

- Defensive Drives: Ever watched Terminator? The U.S. government knows the importance of having Artificial Intelligence (AI) on its side rather than a Skynet scenario.

- Tech Leadership: The birthplace of Apple and Google has its eyes on the Artificial Intelligence (AI) crown.

THE US STRATEGY INCLUDES:

- Academic Alliances: Universities like MIT are at the forefront of Artificial Intelligence (AI) research, ensuring a steady stream of innovations.

- Investing in Innovation: By backing Artificial Intelligence (AI) startups, the U.S. ensures it remains a cradle of technological advancement.

- Ethical Endeavors: With open debates on Artificial Intelligence (AI) ethics, the U.S. aims for balanced Artificial Intelligence (AI) growth.

US CHALLENGES INCLUDE:

- Balancing innovation with regulation. With great power comes great... congressional hearings.

THE GREAT WALL OF MACHINE LEARNING (ML): CHINA

The Middle Kingdom is making no secret of its ambitions. By 2030, China aims to be the world's premier Artificial Intelligence (AI) innovation center. And if their progress so far is any indication, they might get there.

THE GOALS OF CHINA INCLUDE:

- Artificial Intelligence (AI) Supremacy: China's not just aiming for a slice of the Artificial Intelligence (AI) pie. They want the whole bakery.

- Economic Evolution: Through Artificial Intelligence (AI), China aims to upgrade its vast manufacturing sector and move towards a tech-centric economy.

- Smartification: That's not a typo! China plans to use Artificial Intelligence (AI) to create "smart cities."

THE CHINA STRATEGY INCLUDES:

- State Support: China's top-down approach means the government is deeply involved in Artificial Intelligence (AI) growth.

- Data Deluge: With a massive population using digital services, China has data, the raw material for Artificial Intelligence (AI), in spades.

- Education Emphasis: Artificial Intelligence (AI) is becoming part of the curriculum from school to university.

CHINA'S CHALLENGES INCLUDE:

- Intellectual property concerns and global trust issues. Plus, the ever-looming question of Artificial Intelligence (AI) ethics.

THE ETHICAL ENTHUSIASTS: EUROPEAN UNION (EU)

The European Union (EU) might seem like a slow mover, but they're more the "slow and steady wins the race" type. With a focus on ethics and regulations, they're ensuring Artificial Intelligence (AI) serves everyone (with a side of croissants and bratwurst).

THE GOALS OF THE EUROPEAN UNION (EU) INCLUDE:

- Ethical Artificial Intelligence (AI): The European Union (EU) wants to lead in creating Artificial Intelligence (AI) that's as ethical as it's effective.

- Economic Enhancement: The old continent seeks a new lease on life by riding the Artificial Intelligence (AI) wave.

- Citizen-Centric Services: Using Artificial Intelligence (AI) to make lives better? That's the EU's motto.

THE EUROPEAN UNION (EU) STRATEGY INCLUDES:

- Regulatory Frameworks: The General Data Protection Regulation (GDPR) was just their warm-up act. The European Union (EU) is all about setting global Artificial Intelligence (AI) standards.

- Inter-country Collaborations: Neighbors sharing sugar? Outdated. Neighbors sharing Artificial Intelligence (AI) research? Just European Union (EU) things.

- Innovation Incubation: Research hubs and grants are aplenty in the EU to foster Artificial Intelligence (AI) growth.

EUROPEAN UNION (EU) CHALLENGES INCLUDE:

- Striking a balance between 27 member states can be, well, a tad tricky.

THE AI TSARS: RUSSIA

Russia, the land of matryoshka dolls and vodka, might seem chilly, but their Artificial Intelligence (AI) aspirations are heating up!

THE GOALS OF RUSSIA INCLUDE:

- Defensive Dominance: In the great Russian winters, they're looking for some Artificial Intelligence (AI) warmth.

- Tech Prestige: Global recognition in Artificial Intelligence (AI) is Russia's modern-day "moon landing."

THE RUSSIAN STRATEGY INCLUDES:

- Military Machine Learning (ML): Fusing Artificial Intelligence (AI) with defense is top of the list.

- Education Emphasis: Russia's gearing up its youth for the Artificial Intelligence (AI) era, one algorithm at a time.

RUSSIA'S CHALLENGES INCLUDE:

- Limited commercial applications and economic sanctions have put a bit of a damper on expansive collaborations.

THE DIGITAL DESI (DEVELOP, EMPOWER, AND SYNERGIZE INDIA) DRIVE: INDIA

With a booming IT sector and a plethora of tech talent, India is spicing things up in the AI realm!

THE GOALS OF INDIA INCLUDE:

- Tech Transformation: Moving from being the IT back-office to the Artificial Intelligence (AI) front-runner.

- Social Solutions: Harnessing Artificial Intelligence (AI) to solve age-old problems, from agriculture to transportation.

THE INDIA STRATEGY INCLUDES:

- Startup Surge: Bangalore is no longer just "The Garden City." It's India's Silicon Valley.

- Global Collaborations: India's playing the perfect host to global Artificial Intelligence (AI) giants and their R&D centers.

INDIA'S CHALLENGES INCLUDE:

- Infrastructure and funding hurdles. But with a chai in hand, they're marching on!

BITES FROM AROUND THE WORLD:

Canada: is becoming a hotspot for Artificial Intelligence (AI) research, eh! Universities like Toronto and Montreal are producing top-tier Artificial Intelligence (AI) research.

Israel: might be small, but when it comes to Artificial Intelligence (AI) innovation, it's truly the startup nation with Artificial Intelligence (AI)-driven cybersecurity solutions.

South Korea: isn't just about K-pop and kimchi; they're heavily investing in Artificial Intelligence (AI) R&D, eyeing industries like healthcare and entertainment.

Across the board, countries seem to follow a few common strategies. Education and Talent Cultivation: From introducing AI in school curriculums to setting up specialized universities, nations understand that the brainy folks will drive this revolution. Public-Private Partnerships: Governments are joining hands with companies to fast-track innovation. After all, two brains (or a million) are better than one! Ethics and Regulations: As Uncle Ben in Spider-Man once said, "With great power comes great responsibility." Countries are crafting guidelines to ensure AI doesn't run amok.

IN SUMMARY: PUT ON YOUR RUNNING SHOES!

The Artificial Intelligence (AI) race is on, and it's more of a relay than a sprint. Countries are not just competing; they're collaborating, innovating, and setting the pace for a future where Artificial Intelligence (AI) is omnipresent.

It's a thrilling time in the world of Artificial Intelligence (AI)! Nations across the globe are hopping onto the Artificial Intelligence (AI) bandwagon, each with its own flair and strategy. While some are sprinting ahead, others are taking the scenic route, savoring every byte and bot.

As Artificial Intelligence (AI) continues to shape our world, it'll be fascinating to see how these national narratives unfold. Will they collaborate or compete? Only time (and perhaps a future ChatGPT version) will tell.

As we wrap up our Artificial Intelligence (AI) world tour, remember the Artificial Intelligence (AI) journey isn't about the destination but the adventures along the way. So, until our next digital escapade, stay curious stay techie!

Next, we explore how Artificial Intelligence (AI) transforms sectors from medicine to music and the delightful (sometimes bizarre) intersections of man, machine, and daily life. Stay tuned, and always remember to back up your data (because, you know, Artificial Intelligence (AI) isn't perfect)!

CHAPTER 11

"INTO THE ARTIFICIAL INTELLIGENCE (AI)VERSE" – REAL-WORLD APPLICATIONS AND EXAMPLES

In the vast expanse of our universe, we've unearthed a parallel dimension, the "Artificial Intelligence (AI)Verse," if you will. This realm isn't filled with galaxies, stars, or planets; instead, it's teeming with algorithms, codes, and data. Artificial Intelligence (AI)'s reach has expanded far beyond those old sci-fi tales, embedding itself into the very fabric of our daily existence. So, buckle up as we traverse this Artificial Intelligence (AI)-driven universe and unveil how Artificial Intelligence (AI) reshapes industries, from healthcare to Hollywood.

SPECIFIC SIMPLE EXAMPLES OF ARTIFICIAL INTELLIGENCE (AI)

First, let's explore a few straightforward Artificial Intelligence (AI) examples. Following that, we'll delve further into its potential industry applications.

- **IBM Watson:** Originally known for its victory on the game show "Jeopardy!", it's a suite of Artificial Intelligence (AI) tools and applications used for data analysis, healthcare, and more.

- **Google DeepMind's AlphaGo:** This Artificial Intelligence (AI) system defeated the world champion Go player, marking a significant achievement in Artificial Intelligence (AI)'s ability to manage complex tasks.

- **OpenAI's GPT (Generative Pre-trained Transformer):** A language model designed to generate human-like text based on the input it receives.

- **Tesla's Autopilot:** An advanced driver-assistance system with features that provide semi-autonomous driving capabilities.

- **Amazon's Alexa:** A virtual assistant Artificial Intelligence (AI) developed by Amazon, primarily used in the Echo and Echo Dot smart speakers.

- **Apple's Siri:** A virtual assistant integrated into Apple devices, helping users with tasks using voice commands.

- **Microsoft's Azure Cognitive Services:** A collection of Artificial Intelligence (AI) services and APIs that help developers build intelligent applications without having direct Artificial Intelligence (AI) or data science skills.

- **NVIDIA's Deep Learning AI:** NVIDIA is known for its Graphics Processing Units (GPUs), but they also provide Deep Learning Artificial Intelligence (AI) and Artificial Intelligence (AI) platforms for various sectors, including gaming, automotive, and healthcare.

- **Chatbots:** Many companies use chatbots for customer service. These programs simulate conversations with users, especially over the Internet.

- **Recommendation Systems:** Used by platforms like Netflix, Spotify, and Amazon, these Artificial Intelligence (AI) systems analyze user preferences and behaviors to recommend movies, music, or products.

Industries Using Artificial (AI)

Now, let's examine some examples specific to certain industries.

MEDICAL MARVELS: ARTIFICIAL INTELLIGENCE (AI) IN HEALTHCARE

Medicine has always been about precision, care, and continuous evolution. Introduce Artificial Intelligence (AI) into this mix, and you get explosive transformative potential.

- **Diagnostics and Imaging**: Remember the game "Spot the Difference"? Well, Artificial Intelligence (AI) can play it better than any human regarding medical images. With Machine Learning, systems can now detect anomalies in X-rays, MRIs, and CT scans, often with better accuracy than human experts.

- **Drug Discovery:** Designing a drug isn't child's play. It requires understanding complex biochemical interactions. Artificial

Intelligence (AI) can sift through vast databases, analyzing molecular structures and predicting their effectiveness against diseases. What once took years now might take months or even weeks.

- **Personalized Treatment:** We all remember that one teacher who catered lessons to each student's needs. Artificial Intelligence (AI) does something similar for patients. By analyzing genetic data, Artificial Intelligence (AI) can recommend treatments tailored to an individual's genetic makeup.

- **Virtual Health Assistants:** "Alexa, why does my stomach hurt after eating?" Artificial Intelligence (AI)-powered health assistants can provide immediate advice, schedule doctor's appointments, or even remind patients to take their medication.

THE SHOW MUST GO ARTIFICIAL INTELLIGENCE (AI): ENTERTAINMENT INDUSTRY

From creating mesmerizing visual effects to composing catchy tunes, Artificial Intelligence (AI) is ready for its close-up in entertainment.

- **Script Analysis:** Believe it or not, Artificial Intelligence (AI) can now analyze scripts, predicting potential box office success or suggesting plot improvements. The next Oscar winner might have an algorithm as its secret weapon!

- **Music Composition:** Think Artificial Intelligence (AI) can't jam? Think again! Platforms today can generate original compositions, whether you want a jazz piece, classical symphony, or even the next pop hit.

- **Video Game Design:** Gamers, rejoice! Artificial Intelligence (AI) can now design complex game environments, adapting in real-time to a player's actions, ensuring every game session is unique.

- **Content Recommendations:** "Because you watched..." Yes, that's Artificial Intelligence (AI) at work, analyzing your preferences and suggesting what you might like next, making binge-watching more addictive.

SHOP 'TIL THE ARTIFICIAL INTELLIGENCE (AI) DROPS: RETAIL AND E-COMMERCE

Next time you add an item to your online shopping cart, remember there's probably an algorithm working behind the scenes.

- **Personalized Shopping Experience:** Based on your browsing habits, purchase history, and even when you hover over products, Artificial Intelligence (AI) tailors a shopping experience just for you.

- **Chatbots & Customer Service:** Got a complaint or a query? Before you reach an actual human, chances are you're chatting with an Artificial Intelligence (AI) bot, guiding you through common problems or helping you track your order.

- **Inventory Management:** No more "out of stock" disappointments. Artificial Intelligence (AI) helps retailers predict which items will fly off the shelves, ensuring they're well-stocked and ready for your shopping spree.

- **Dynamic Pricing:** Have you ever noticed flight prices fluctuating or that special discount just when contemplating a purchase? Artificial Intelligence (AI)'s predictive analysis determines the best price point to maximize sales.

FINANCE: COUNTING MORE THAN JUST MONEY

The world of finance is complex, dynamic, and let's admit it, a tad intimidating. Enter Artificial Intelligence (AI), simplifying, optimizing, and revolutionizing.

- **Fraud Detection:** Artificial Intelligence (AI) systems can analyze millions of transactions per second, flagging suspicious activity. That text you get about a dubious transaction? Yep, Artificial Intelligence (AI)'s got your back (and your wallet).

- **Algorithmic Trading:** Stock markets are unpredictable. Or are they? Artificial Intelligence (AI) algorithms can analyze market trends, news, and even social media sentiments, making informed trading decisions in microseconds.

- **Personal Financial Management:** Budgeting is challenging, but Artificial Intelligence (AI) can help. Apps now analyze spending habits, suggest budgets, and even automatically save money for you.

- **Credit Scoring**: Traditional credit scores can sometimes be unfair or not wholly indicative of one's financial habits. Artificial Intelligence (AI) assesses a broader range of data, from bill payments to online shopping habits, offering a more comprehensive credit analysis.

THE SOCIAL ARTIFICIAL INTELLIGENCE (AI): MEDIA AND CONNECTIVITY

From the posts we see to the ads that pop up, Artificial Intelligence (AI) is the silent orchestrator of our digital lives.

- **Content Filtering:** Ever wonder how your social media feed is curated? Artificial Intelligence (AI) algorithms consider your interactions, likes, shares, and even the duration you gaze at a post to tailor your feed.

- **Face and Voice Recognition:** Tagging friends in photos or unlocking your phone with a glance, Artificial Intelligence (AI)-driven recognition systems make it seamless.

- **Predictive Text and Smart Replies:** "Hey, how are- ... you?" Artificial Intelligence (AI) finishes your sentences, predicts your next word, and even suggests quick replies, making digital conversations faster.

- **Ad Targeting:** It's no coincidence that an ad for the shoes you were eyeing appears on your feed. Artificial Intelligence (AI) analyses your online activity, ensuring advertisers hit the mark more often than not.

A DASH OF FUN: QUIRKIEST ARTIFICIAL INTELLIGENCE (AI) ENCOUNTERS

For all its utility and seriousness, Artificial Intelligence (AI) has its light-hearted moments, too. Let's delve into some of the weirdest and funniest things people have asked voice assistants:

- **"Will you marry me?"** A popular one! Most voice assistants respond with wit, reminding users they're just lines of code.

- **"What should I wear today?"** Some voice assistants might check the weather and offer a practical suggestion, while others might remind you that they need more fashion sense.

- **"Can you laugh?"** Try it. Some Artificial Intelligence (AI) responses are genuinely chuckle-worthy!

- **"What's the meaning of life?"** They don't have the answer but expect a cheeky reply referencing popular culture or philosophy.

IN SUMMARY: EMBRACING OUR ARTIFICIAL INTELLIGENCE (AI) CO-PILOTS

In this whirlwind tour of the Artificial Intelligence (AI)Verse, one thing stands clear – Artificial Intelligence (AI) isn't just about futuristic robots or high-tech labs. It's interwoven into our lives, reshaping experiences, industries, and possibilities.

Yet, as we marvel at Artificial Intelligence (AI)'s vast capabilities, let's also cherish the human touch, the intuition, and the emotions that machines can't replicate. After all, Artificial Intelligence (AI) is an incredibly sophisticated tool, but a tool, nonetheless. We must harness its potential, guide its evolution, and ensure it enriches our world.

As we head into our final chapter, let's dream a little. What lies ahead for Artificial Intelligence (AI)? What wonders (or challenges) await in the next decade? The future beckons, and with Artificial Intelligence (AI) by our side, it's bound to be an exhilarating journey.

CHAPTER 12

"FUTURE BYTES" – WHAT LIES AHEAD FOR ARTIFICIAL INTELLIGENCE, CHATGPT, AND MACHINE LEARNING

"Software that can take in and respond to natural language inputs is a big step in making computers a more intuitive tool."

- Bill Gates, Founder Microsoft

Imagine a world where your Artificial Intelligence (AI) assistant anticipates your every need, even before you realize it yourself. Where self-learning systems orchestrate an entire city's infrastructure, ensuring smooth traffic, optimal energy consumption, and public safety. Or where the line between human creativity and machine-generated content becomes so blurred that you can't tell the difference. Sound too futuristic? Not in the fast-paced world of Artificial Intelligence (AI)!

Today, we stand on the brink of a technological renaissance. The seeds we've sown in Artificial Intelligence (AI), ChatGPT, and Machine

Learning (ML) are about to bear fruit beyond our wildest imaginations. Let's journey into the not-so-distant future and explore what might await.

A SYMPHONY OF SENSES: MULTIMODAL ARTIFICIAL INTELLIGENCE (AI)

- Today's Artificial Intelligence (AI) systems primarily interact through text or voice. In the future, multimodal Artificial Intelligence (AI) will synthesize information from various sources – voice, text, images, videos, and emotions. Imagine a system that can watch a movie, analyze its script, listen to the soundtrack, and then generate a comprehensive review. Or think of an Artificial Intelligence (AI) personal shopper that observes your reactions via a webcam, reads your past purchase history, listens to your voice, and then suggests the perfect outfit for your next big event.

- **Prediction:** With the convergence of different Artificial Intelligence (AI) models and techniques, multi-sensory Artificial Intelligence (AI) systems will become ubiquitous, offering richer, more human-like interactions.

REINVENTING EDUCATION: PERSONAL ARTIFICIAL INTELLIGENCE (AI) TUTORS

- Why settle for a one-size-fits-all curriculum when an Artificial Intelligence (AI)-powered tutor can curate a personalized learning journey? These systems will recognize students' strengths, weaknesses, preferences, and pace. Are you struggling with algebra but passionate about history? Artificial Intelligence (AI) will adjust accordingly, ensuring academic success and a love for learning.

- **Prediction:** Within a decade, Artificial Intelligence (AI)-driven education will democratize learning, making high-quality education accessible to all, irrespective of geographical or economic barriers.

THE PINNACLE OF PERSONALIZATION: ARTIFICIAL INTELLIGENCE (AI) FOR MENTAL AND PHYSICAL WELL-BEING

- While wearables that monitor physical health are already mainstream, imagine Artificial Intelligence (AI) systems that can detect emotional fluctuations, offering real-time interventions. Have you had a rough day at work? Your Artificial Intelligence (AI) can suggest relaxation techniques, play your favorite calming tunes, or even recommend a heartwarming movie.

- **Prediction:** Beyond mere monitoring, future Artificial Intelligence (AI) will serve as proactive wellness partners, ensuring holistic well-being.

ARTIFICIAL INTELLIGENCE (AI)-POWERED CREATIVITY: ART, MUSIC, AND BEYOND

- Artificial Intelligence (AI)'s foray into the creative world has already begun, with algorithms composing music or assisting in film production. In the future, artists and machines might collaborate even more closely. Artificial Intelligence (AI) could suggest a melody for a musician or help a writer overcome writer's block by proposing potential plot developments.

- **Prediction:** Artificial Intelligence (AI) won't replace artists but will become their muse, co-creator, and collaborator, pushing the boundaries of human creativity.

UNIVERSAL TRANSLATORS: BREAKING DOWN LANGUAGE BARRIERS

- With Artificial Intelligence (AI)-driven translation, the world becomes a smaller place. Real-time, context-aware translations will allow for seamless communication, irrespective of linguistic differences. Imagine wearing intelligent glasses that translate foreign signboards in real time or participating in global conferences without ever needing a human translator.

- **Prediction:** The Tower of Babel's barriers will crumble, fostering unparalleled global collaboration and understanding.

MORAL MACHINES: ARTIFICIAL INTELLIGENCE (AI) WITH ETHICAL FOUNDATIONS

- As Artificial Intelligence (AI) systems make more decisions, questions of morality and ethics become paramount. Should an autonomous car prioritize the safety of its passengers over pedestrians? How does Artificial Intelligence (AI) balance personalization with privacy concerns? Future Artificial Intelligence (AI) models might have ethical frameworks embedded, allowing them to navigate complex moral landscapes.

- **Prediction:** Philosophers, ethicists, and technologists will collaborate more closely, ensuring Artificial Intelligence (AI) development aligns with human values.

ARTIFICIAL INTELLIGENCE (AI) DEMOCRACIES: PARTICIPATIVE, INFORMED GOVERNANCE

- Governance and public administration can benefit immensely from Artificial Intelligence (AI). From optimizing urban infrastructures and managing resources efficiently to analyzing public sentiment on policies – Artificial Intelligence (AI) can usher in an era of transparent, responsive, and effective governance.

- **Prediction:** Future governments will actively adopt Artificial Intelligence (AI) as a tool and a cornerstone of participatory democracy.

REVAMPING RESEARCH: ARTIFICIAL INTELLIGENCE (AI) IN SCIENCE AND EXPLORATION

- The universe holds mysteries that human minds alone might never unravel. But with Artificial Intelligence (AI)-assisted research, we can decode complex patterns, whether they're in sub-atomic particles, vast galactic structures, or the intricate web of Earth's ecosystems.

- **Prediction:** The next significant scientific breakthrough, be it in quantum physics, space exploration, or biology, might have an Artificial Intelligence (AI) co-author.

THE EVOLUTION OF ARTIFICIAL INTELLIGENCE (AI) ITSELF: SELF-LEARNING AND AUTONOMY

- Today's Artificial Intelligence (AI) models, impressive as they are, still rely heavily on human guidance. The future might witness Artificial Intelligence (AI) systems that can learn from scratch without needing vast labeled datasets. These systems will be more adaptive, resilient, and capable of navigating unfamiliar situations.

- **Prediction:** True Artificial General Intelligence (AGI) – machines with cognitive capabilities on par with humans – might move from the realm of science fiction to reality.

RESHAPING INDUSTRIES: NEW PROFESSIONS AND PARADIGMS

- Every technological revolution heralds the end of specific jobs and gives birth to new opportunities. As Artificial Intelligence (AI) automates routine tasks, the human workforce will shift towards roles emphasizing creativity, empathy, and complex problem-solving.

- **Prediction:** Future job markets won't just be about skills but will place a premium on adaptability, lifelong learning, and human-centric values.

IN SUMMARY: BRIDGING BYTES AND HEARTBEATS

As we hurtle towards this promising future, let's remember the essence of our journey. In all its glory, Artificial Intelligence (AI) serves one primary purpose – to augment, enrich, and elevate the human experience. It's not a replacement but a partner, amplifying our potential.

As we've seen, Artificial Intelligence (AI)'s "trendiness" isn't just a passing phase. It's a transformative force, reshaping our present and sculpting our future. While challenges await, so do unprecedented opportunities. The Artificial Intelligence (AI)Verse beckons, and it's a universe where stars, galaxies, and dreams converge.

Here's to the future, Artificial Intelligence (AI), and the infinite potential of bytes and heartbeats intertwined!

EPILOGUE

"ARTIFICIAL INTELLIGENCE, HUMANS, AND THE AGE-OLD QUEST FOR THE OFF SWITCH"

As we wind down our extraordinary journey through the riveting world of Artificial Intelligence (AI), it's time to take a breather, stretch out those human limbs, and have a little fun. After all, we've navigated through Neural Networks, conversed with ChatGPT, delved deep into the Artificial Intelligence (AI)Verse, and peeked into the tantalizing future of Artificial Intelligence (AI). If that isn't cause for a small celebration, I don't know what is!

A MACHINE'S NIGHT OUT:

- Imagine if your Artificial Intelligence (AI)-powered devices decided to take the night off. Siri's singing karaoke with Alexa, Google Assistant is cracking jokes, and your Roomba? Well, it's doing the robot dance, of course! While this seems far-fetched, it underscores a critical point: Artificial Intelligence (AI), for all its sophistication, is still a tool we've created. It doesn't need time off or a social life, but we humans sure do!

- **Lesson:** Remember to unplug, both literally and figuratively. Don't let the allure of technology rob you of life's simple pleasures.

A HUMAN'S GUIDE TO OUTSMARTING ARTIFICIAL INTELLIGENCE (AI):

- It's game night! You versus your Artificial Intelligence (AI) chess program. It's been beating you for weeks, but you have a strategy tonight. You decide to...play entirely randomly! No system, no logic, just whimsical moves. And guess what? Your Artificial Intelligence (AI) opponent is utterly bamboozled. Sometimes, human unpredictability is our greatest strength.

- **Lesson:** Embrace your quirks, whims, and sudden desires to eat ice cream in winter. It's what makes you uniquely human.

THE ARTIFICIAL INTELLIGENCE (AI)-POWERED ROMANCE:

- We joked about ChatGPT's dating profile earlier, but let's extrapolate. In a world where Artificial Intelligence (AI) can analyze and predict human emotions, what if an Artificial Intelligence (AI) matchmaker existed?

"Based on your search history, love for 80s rock, and an inexplicable fondness for pineapple on pizza, we've found a 99.9% compatibility match!"

- **Lesson:** While algorithms might find a match, love is beautifully irrational. It's not about compatibility percentages but those inexplicable butterflies in the stomach.

COOKING WITH ARTIFICIAL INTELLIGENCE (AI) – THE TOO MANY COOKS SCENARIO:

- Imagine using multiple Artificial Intelligence (AI) assistants in the kitchen. Siri sets the oven temperature, Google Assistant reads the recipe, and Alexa plays your cooking tunes. But whoops! It would help if you remembered who does what; chaos ensues, and you end up with a charred version of what was supposed to be pasta.

- **Lesson:** Tech is a fabulous sous-chef but remember who's the head chef in your kitchen (and life).

THE ULTIMATE FITNESS CHALLENGE: HUMAN VS. ROBOT:

- Let's say you challenge a humanoid robot to a race in the not-so-distant future. It's designed to replicate human movements, so it's fair game. The race starts, and your neck and neck. But halfway through, the robot's battery dies. Victory is yours!

- **Lesson:** Endurance and resilience are human traits. Whether it's a marathon, life's challenges, or a sudden downpour without an umbrella, we find a way to keep going.

ARTIFICIAL INTELLIGENCE (AI)'S EXISTENTIAL CRISIS: TO BE OR NOT TO BE...PROGRAMMED:

- It's a quiet night, and you decide to chat with your Artificial Intelligence (AI). You ask it about the meaning of life. After a pause, it says, "Well, for you, it might be happiness, experiences, or maybe 42. For me, it's efficient algorithms and error-free code."

- **Lesson:** Each of us, human or machine, has a purpose. Find yours, and don't let anyone (or any Artificial Intelligence (AI)) define it for you.

AN ARTIFICIAL INTELLIGENCE (AI)'S DAY OFF – OH WAIT, THAT'S NOT A THING!

- In a hilarious twist, your Artificial Intelligence (AI) sends you a message: "Taking the day off. Need some downtime." You chuckle, realizing it's a prank by a family member. But it gets you thinking. What does relaxation mean for a machine? A system update?

- **Lesson:** Rest and relaxation are vital. If machines had emotions, they'd envy our ability to lounge on a couch and do nothing.

THE CLASSIC "TURN IT OFF AND ON AGAIN":

- In a world increasingly dominated by tech, the oldest trick in the book still stands. When in doubt, reboot. Is your sophisticated Artificial Intelligence (AI) system giving you sass? A good ol' restart might be the solution.

- **Lesson:** Sometimes, simplicity trumps sophistication. Remember the basics.

WHEN ARTIFICIAL INTELLIGENCE (AI) TRIES COMEDY:

- You ask your voice assistant to tell you a joke. It responds, "Why did the algorithm go to therapy? It had too many loops!" You chuckle, but there's a realization. Artificial Intelligence (AI) can generate jokes based on data, but genuine humor? That's a human trait.

- **Lesson:** Our imperfections, nuances, and varied experiences make humor rich and diverse. Celebrate them.

THE GRAND FINALE: THE SYMPHONY OF MAN AND MACHINE:

- Picture this: An auditorium, a grand stage, and two performers – a human pianist and an Artificial Intelligence (AI)-powered robot. They play a duet, a blend of classical melodies, and algorithmically generated tunes. It's harmonious, mesmerizing, and a testament to the magic that happens when man and machine collaborate.

- **Lesson:** The future isn't about Artificial Intelligence (AI) vs. Humans. It's about how we can co-create, innovate, and elevate experiences when we work together.

IN CONCLUSION:

As we wrap up this enlightening expedition, remember that there's a touch of humanity at the heart of every line of code, algorithm, and machine-learning model. Artificial Intelligence (AI) mirrors our aspirations, ingenuity, and, sometimes, our quirks.

So, as we step into this brave new world, remember to embrace both the machine's precision and the human's passion. After all, in this dance of bytes and emotions, the missteps, improvisations, and unexpected twirls make the journey worthwhile.

And to end on a light note – if ever in doubt, if ever overwhelmed, remember the universal solution: "Have you tried turning it off and on again?"

Here's to a future brimming with promise, laughter, and whimsy! Cheers!

APPENDIX

KEY TERMS AND DEFINITIONS

Here are 50 key terms related to Artificial Intelligence (AI), ChatGPT, and Machine Learning (ML), accompanied by their definitions:

- **Activation Function**: A function in a Neural Network that defines the output of a neuron given a set of inputs.

- **Artificial General Intelligence (AGI)**: A type of Artificial Intelligence (AI) that possesses the ability to understand, learn, and apply knowledge in a wide variety of tasks at a level comparable to human intelligence.

- **Algorithm**: A set of rules or procedures programmed into a computer to solve specific problems or accomplish a task.

- **Artificial Intelligence (AI)**: The science of creating machines capable of performing tasks that usually require human intelligence.

- **Attention Mechanism**: A component in Neural Networks, particularly transformers, allows the model to focus on specific parts of the input data.

- **Autoencoder**: A Neural Network used for unsupervised learning of efficient encodings, often for dimensionality reduction or anomaly detection.

- **Backpropagation**: A training method used for adjusting the weights of neurons based on the error rate of the output.

- **Bagging**: An ensemble method that involves training multiple instances of the same model on different subsets of the data.

- **Batch Size**: The number of training examples utilized in one iteration.

- **Bias in Machine Learning (ML)**: Unwanted and often systematic discrepancies in data or algorithm outputs can lead to unfair or discriminatory results.

- **Boosting**: An ensemble method that trains models sequentially, each trying to correct its predecessor's mistakes.

- **ChatGPT**: A model by OpenAI that uses Generative Pre-trained Transformers (GPT) to simulate human-like conversation.

- **Clustering**: An unsupervised learning technique to group similar data points based on specific features.

- **Convolutional Neural Network (CNN)**: A Deep Learning algorithm primarily used for image processing and recognition.

- **Data Augmentation**: Techniques used to increase the amount of training data, like rotating or cropping images.

- **Deep Learning**: A subset of Machine Learning (ML) utilizing multiple layers of Neural Networks to analyze different data factors.

- **Decision Trees**: Supervised learning models used for classification and regression, representing decisions as branches.

- **Embeddings**: Representations of discrete data, like words, in continuous vector space, enabling mathematical operations.

- **Ensemble Methods**: Techniques combining multiple models' decisions to improve overall performance, such as bagging or boosting.

- **Epoch**: One complete forward and backward pass of all the training data through a Neural Network.

- **Feature Extraction**: The process of selecting or transforming variables from raw data to better model the underlying patterns.

- **Fine-tuning**: Adjusting a pre-trained model to a new task by further training it on new data.

- **Generative Adversarial Network (GAN)**: A type of Neural Network setup where two networks, the generator and discriminator, are trained simultaneously through adversarial processes.

- **Gradient Descent**: An optimization algorithm used to minimize the value of the loss function by adjusting model parameters.

- **Hyperparameter**: Parameters set before training a Machine Learning (ML) model, like learning rate or batch size.

- **Inference Engine**: The component of an Artificial Intelligence (AI) system that applies logic rules to knowledge, drawing new conclusions.

- **Learning Rate**: A hyperparameter determines the step size at each iteration while moving towards a minimum in the loss function.

- **Loss Function**: A method of evaluating how well an algorithm models the given data. A lower value indicates a better fit.

- **Machine Learning (ML)**: A branch of Artificial Intelligence (AI) where computers learn from data to improve performance without explicitly being programmed for specific tasks.

- **Natural Language Processing (NLP)**: The intersection of Artificial Intelligence (AI) and linguistics that enables machines to understand, interpret, and produce human language.

- **Neural Network**: Computational structures inspired by the human brain's neurons, designed to recognize patterns from data.

- **Overfitting**: When a Machine Learning (ML) model tailors itself too closely to training data, performing poorly on unfamiliar data.

- **Perceptron**: A binary classification algorithm and a type of artificial neuron in Neural Network architecture.

- **Principal Component Analysis (PCA)**: A method for reducing data dimensionality while retaining as much variability as possible.

- **Random Forest**: An ensemble method that creates a 'forest' of decision trees and outputs the mode of the classes or means prediction.

- **Recurrent Neural Network (RNN)**: Neural Networks are designed to recognize patterns in data sequences, such as time series or natural language.

- **Regularization**: Techniques to prevent overfitting by adding penalties to the loss function.

- **Reinforcement Learning**: Machine Learning (ML) technique where algorithms learn by taking actions and receiving rewards or penalties based on those actions.

- **Semantics**: In Artificial Intelligence (AI) and Natural Language Processing (NLP), this refers to the study of meaning in language.

- **Sequence-to-Sequence Models**: Neural architectures designed for tasks where input and output sequences can be of different lengths, standard in translation or summarization.

- **Supervised Learning**: Machine Learning (ML) method where the model is trained using both input data and its corresponding correct output.

- **Support Vector Machine (SVM)**: A supervised Machine Learning (ML) algorithm that can be used for both classification and regression challenges.

- **Tokenization**: The process of converting text into individual elements or "tokens" for processing, usually in Natural Language Processing (NLP).

- **Transfer Learning**: Leveraging a pre-trained model on a new related task, saving training time and resources.

- **Transformer Architecture**: A Neural Network design often used in Natural Language Processing (NLP) tasks, introducing the attention mechanism to weigh input data differently.

- **Turing Test**: An evaluation of a machine's ability to exhibit intelligent behavior indistinguishable from a human.

- **Underfitting**: When a model is too simple to capture underlying patterns in the data.

- **Unsupervised Learning**: Machine Learning (ML) method where the algorithm identifies patterns in data without referring to known or labeled outcomes.

- **Validation Data**: Data used to fine-tune model parameters and prevent overfitting during training.

AN ODE TO HUMANS, MACHINES, AND THAT STUBBORN WI-FI SIGNAL

"In the vast galaxy of creation, between the realms of ones and zeros, there lies a space filled with gratitude. This is where my acknowledgments reside."

– Probably some Artificial Intelligence poet shortly

To Motherboard and Father Processor: First and foremost, a massive shoutout to the fundamental building blocks of the tech world. Without you, none of this would have been possible. Literally.

Java, Python, C++, and the Gang: I'd like to thank the programming languages that were the backbone for much of our discussion. You've been the true MVPs, even when your error messages made me question my life choices.

Dear Human Brain: For being the gold standard that Artificial Intelligence (AI) aspires to emulate and for processing countless cans of Red Bull into coherent sentences. You're the original Neural Network, and you're fabulous.

Every Device That Patiently Waited: To the laptops that didn't crash and the voice assistants who played the perfect tunes during late-night writing sessions – thank you.

The Internet: For is a vast reservoir of information. And to my Wi-Fi – even though you chose to play hard to get sometimes, our love-hate relationship strengthened this book. You truly tested the limits of my "turn it off and on again" theory.

ChatGPT & Fellow Artificial Intelligence (AI)s: Thank you for the intriguing conversations, the perfectly timed jokes, and the occasional reminders of how human I truly am, especially when faced with your rapid-fire calculations.

My Support System: Friends, family, and that bartender who knew my drink by heart – thank you for the encouragement and the understanding nods when I rambled about algorithms.

To You, Dear Reader: For embarking on this journey with me. For laughing at the jokes (or at least pretending to), pondering the ethical dilemmas, and embracing the world of Artificial Intelligence (AI) with open arms and an open mind.

There's a place for humor, gratitude, and humanity in the maze of binary decisions and complex computations. Thank you for being part of this narrative from the depths of my organic (and occasionally error-prone) heart.

May your algorithms always be efficient, your data clean, and your devices forever compatible with the latest updates. Until our next digital adventure!

-John Binks